KEEP GOING!

Edited by Ken Todd

Keep Going!

ENCOURAGEMENT FOR CHRISTIAN MINISTRY

the columba press

First published in 2000 by

the columba press

55A Spruce Avenue, Stillorgan Industrial Park, Blackrock, Co Dublin

Cover by Bill Bolger
Origination by The Columba Press
Printed in Ireland by ColourBooks Ltd, Dublin

ISBN 1 85607 294 0

Contents

Introduction

I am among you as one who serves (Lk 22:27)

We forget that the Church of Jesus Christ is an every-member ministry. Every Christian is called to be a Christopher, a 'Christ-bearer'. Ministry is service and Christians are indeed saved to serve following the example and command of Jesus. Jesus demonstrated and taught that service is the hallmark of all Christian ministry.

A good biblical example of this is in Mark 1:29-31 when Jesus healed Peter's mother-in-law. Mark uses it as a paradigm of the gospel experience. Note the sequence of events that together become an illustration of the gospel in our lives. The woman is in the power of death, friends intercede for her, the Son of God strongly takes hold of her and raises her up, she sits with him, the forces of evil are put to flight, the woman rises to engage in grateful service, as a consequence many more people come to Jesus for salvation.

Here at the beginning of his 'busy' gospel, Mark is setting out his stall to demonstrate that following Jesus leads to active service. When Jesus calls disciples it is with the words: 'Come, follow me and I will make you …' (1:17). Being a follower of Jesus is not so much about what I give to him but about what he gives to me. People who see themselves as clay in the nail-scarred hands of the divine potter are joyfully content to offer 'make me' prayers. The Prodigal Son returned home with his prepared speech proclaiming his unworthiness and a desire: 'make me as one of your servants'. Tagore prayed beautifully: 'O God, make my life simple and straight like a reed for you to fill with music.' Francis of Assisi only wanted to be made like a channel.

At the baptism of Jesus (Mk 1:11) the voice from heaven in-

cluded a quotation from Isaiah 42:1 about the Servant of the
Lord in whom God is well pleased. Jesus regarded himself in the
light of the Servant songs of Isaiah 40-55 where the whole of the
people of God, the nation, is called to be the Servant of the Lord.
Michael Green points out that 'The three themes of utter obedience, fearless witness and innocent suffering, which marked the
Old Testament conception of the Servant of the Lord, run
through the ministry of Jesus.' No wonder Israel turned its back
on the idea and the church is reluctant to take it on board.

How easily the church has been diverted from servanthood! I
suppose it is a crumb of comfort to know that even the first disciples squabbled over preferment when they disputed about the
best seats in the kingdom. Jesus then had to say: 'For even the
Son of Man did not come to be served, but to serve' (Mk 10:45).

How did we acquire the honorific titles that abide and
abound in the church and speak of Lords rather than servants?
Even some of my humble friends who contribute to this book
have had thrust upon them, very unwillingly, superior titles. In
the New Testament church titles tended to be functional rather
than hierarchical. The whole concept of monarchy and hierarchy
in the church has more to do with Constantine than it has with
Christ. I sense that the egalitarianism of this age will see less attention to such titles and it will be no bad thing. It is a diversion
from the servanthood of the towel-girded Servant-King who
washed his disciples' feet and demonstrated the shocking idea
that greatness is measured in terms of service. T. W. Manson
writes: 'In the kingdom of God, service is not a stepping stone to
nobility; it is nobility, the only kind of nobility that is recognised.'

Another diversion from the servanthood of the New
Testament has been the clerical captivity of the church where we
have ministry with a capital 'M' for the ordained. We have allowed ministry to be institutionalised, forgetting that church is a
body of volunteers where every Christian is a minister/servant.
One of the stumbling blocks to greater collaboration between
churches today is the dispute over recognition of ministries and

validity of orders. While there is clear evidence in the New Testament for what is known as the ordained ministry, nowhere in the New Testament is there a priestly caste. All Christians are the laity of God (1 Pet 2:10) and all Christians are ministers of God (see Rom 12 and 1 Cor 12). I hope these chapters will encourage faithful service for Christ.

Footnote

If Jesus is the Servant, then we, like Peter, must let Jesus be our Servant. In the upper room, when washing the proud disciple's feet, Peter refused until Jesus said: 'Unless I wash you, you have no part with me' (Jn 13:8). Having allowed the Lord to serve and thereby save us, we will evermore become his glad servants.

'Yet shall I praise him!'

Peter C. Graves

2 Corinthians 4:1, 7-10

v.1. 'Therefore, since it is by God's mercy that we are engaged in this ministry, we do not lose heart.

v.7. ... we have this treasure in clay jars, so that it may be made clear that this extraordinary power belongs to God and does not come from us.

v.8. we are afflicted in every way, but not crushed; perplexed but not driven to despair,

v.9. persecuted but not forsaken; struck down but not destroyed;

v.10. always carrying in the body the death of Jesus, so that the life of Jesus may also be made visible in our bodies.

Introduction

There is on the Bayeux Tapestry a picture of a man on horseback waving a club in the air, driving forward a group of weary soldiers. Underneath are the words: 'Bishop Odo encouraging the young men.' With these words Dr Gordon Rupp began the sermon he preached at my ordination. He said he wanted to encourage us as we began our ministry.

I also want to encourage you. I know that if I had my life over again, I would still be a minister, for there is no greater privilege. Nevertheless I must confess that at times I do feel the beat of the club more than the words of encouragement. It is not easy to engage in ministry today. Our Western secularised culture is not gospel-friendly. The speed of change makes our people feel threatened and vulnerable. For all the hard work we do, we often don't feel appreciated, and still experience decline. At times we wonder, 'Mother is it worth it?', or to put it in the vernacular, we feel 'clobbered'.

11

1) The way of the Master

There is though nothing new in this. It was the way of the
Master. We follow a crucified Lord, who called his disciples to
take up the cross and follow him. We were never promised an
easy life, but were rather offered 'blood, sweat and tears' – to
quote Garibaldi.

History is full of wounded heroes who were prepared to suffer rather than deny their Lord, and many still suffer today.
Indeed, it has been well said that the growth of the church has
been nurtured on the blood of the martyrs.

Paul certainly knew what it meant to suffer for his faith and
vocation, and this is reflected in the verses of our text. Often
mocked by the crowds, opposed by the Jews, and misunderstood by the very Christians who should have been his staunchest
allies, he still persevered. Ever troubled by the unknown problem he called his 'thorn in the flesh', he stood firm, even in
prison, and in the end he suffered the death of a martyr. When
therefore he says, 'We are afflicted in every way, but not crushed,
perplexed, but not driven to despair; persecuted, but not forsaken;
struck down, but not destroyed', we listen to him. After all, he
did not learn such things from a textbook. They were discovered
on the anvil of human experience.

For Paul the pattern of discipleship, and ministry, was always that of Jesus. It may well involve suffering and finish up in
crucifixion, but from it all comes resurrection. This is perhaps most
clearly seen in the great hymn to Christ quoted in Phil 2:6-11. He
challenges us to 'let the same mind be in you that was in Christ
Jesus'. He willingly surrendered the privileges of heaven, humbled himself and became human, suffered and died. Yet in his
resurrection and ascension, God exalted him, so that 'every
tongue should confess that Jesus Christ is Lord, to the glory of
God the Father.

No wonder Paul could say 'engaged in this ministry, we do
not lose heart'. He knew that for all the appearances to the con-
trary, evil could never ultimately hold the upper hand. The victory had already been won in Christ, and his resurrection. The

troubles are bound to come. It will often seem as though the bottom has dropped out of our world, yet shall we praise him. No matter what happens, his is the victory, therefore we will not lose heart.

2) Never victims, always survivors!

Some face their problems as victims. It is always circumstances that have prevented them achieving their objectives. 'If only' this or that hadn't happened, everything would be all right. I didn't really stand a chance. I'm a victim.

Others determine to be survivors. The problems may be great, but they are seen as opportunities for growth, and so must be faced with courage and determination. Then, with the help of God, the way through is found and victory achieved. This was the approach of Paul. He was a survivor, and those who take the gospel seriously are called to be the same.

Outside the Metropolitan United Methodist Church in Detroit, there is a statue of a young man who had obviously been through very hard times. Behind him is the form of a dragon, trying to hold him back. His face is turned upward, and his smile reflects a deep inner confidence and hope. Carved at the base are the words: 'I shall yet praise him.' It was carved by Gutzon Borglum who is best known for his carving of the faces of four presidents on Mount Rushmore. At a particularly difficult time in his life, when everything seemed to be going wrong, he went to Metropolitan Church and heard Dr Merton Rice preach a sermon entitled 'Yet shall I praise him.' He was so moved and helped by it, that he carved the statue as a gift to the minister.

This statue embodies the faith that inspired Paul to keep going. He constantly stresses that ministry is not done in our own strength. Indeed the longer we minister, the more we realise how dependent we are on God alone. We rely not on our gifts, but on his grace. We are just clay vessels, all too easily prone to break under pressure. But God can and does speak through our vulnerability. He uses us as a channel through whom others can experience his love.

Henri Nouwen speaks of the 'wounded healer', and that is our calling. It's as we humbly accept our woundedness and frailty, and offer it up to God, that we become open to him. Then he moulds and transforms us into his likeness, and uses us to help others.

There was a time when George Frederick Handel was beset with great troubles. His health and fortune had reached their lowest ebb. His right side was paralysed and creditors threatened him with imprisonment. He was tempted to give up, but obedience to God welled up within him and he determined to carry on. It was at this time he wrote his famous *Messiah* which of course includes within it, *The Hallelujah Chorus*. It's as if he is saying, 'My problems may be enormous, but God is bigger still. The Lord will see me through, and I shall praise him. I'm not a victim, I'm a survivor – Hallelujah!

Conclusion

And so, be encouraged. Be strengthened to face the challenge ahead. Never lose heart. The going may be tough, but God is tougher still, and it is he who calls you to be a survivor, not just a victim. Although called to take up our cross to follow the master, we do so in the assurance of resurrection. It may be a Good Friday world, but we are Easter People!

Once the Communists took power in China, he was arrested, and sent to prison. For twenty-three years he endured a regime of forced labour in the frozen borderlands with the Soviet Union. Of course there were many times when he was tempted to give up, but through them all, he refused to deny his Lord. He stood firm in his Christian faith. It was deeply moving to hear him tell his story. At the end of it I asked: 'Is your faith stronger now?' With a radiant smile, he replied, 'Of course, God doesn't let you down!'

Prayer:

Jesus, I fain would find
Thy zeal for God in me,
Thy yearning pity for mankind,
Thy burning charity.

In me thy spirit dwell;
In me thy mercies move:
So shall the fervour of my zeal
Be thy pure flame of love.
Charles Wesley

Mission in Christ's way

Norman W. Taggart

John 20:19-25

Here in John, as in the other gospels, the words of the risen Lord
are in direct response to the disciples' needs. But words by
themselves – even his words – are never enough. What is required, for the disciples and for us, is an encounter with the
risen Lord and the Spirit. Christmas, Easter and Pentecost together provide a springboard for Christian life and mission. The
risen Lord and the Holy Spirit ensure an ever-flowing stream of
joy, energy and zeal for mission. Drawing on the passage, I
make four points about the risen Christ.

The Crucified Christ

The risen Christ is the crucified Christ. 'Jesus came and stood
among them.' He spoke to them and 'showed them his (pierced)
hands and side' (vv. 19, 20). Here was no figment of their imagi-
nation, no ghost, no disembodied spirit, but the risen, crucified
Christ. If there were lingering doubts in their minds, his pierced
hands and side removed them. His wounds were his credentials.
There was a reason for Thomas's later words. He had not been
with the others when Jesus appeared. Their words of witness
did not convince him. 'Unless I see the nail marks in his hands
and put my finger where the nails were,'he protested, 'I will not
believe' (v. 25).

   In the legend of St Martin, Satan appeared in the form of the
risen Christ to Martin and commanded that he worship him.
Martin, however, was suspicious. Hesitating, he looked intently
at the figure's raised hand and cried out, 'No, I cannot worship
you. I do not see the marks of the nails.'

   Christian mission has too often been seen in triumphalist

terms. An indifferent, sceptical and hostile world has the right to look for the marks of sacrificial love when examining our Christian witness and service.

The Comforting Christ

The risen Christ is the comforting Christ. When the doors were locked for fear of the Jews, he came (v. 19). The fear of the disciples was understandable. Their leader had been killed by determined and resourceful enemies. His followers might well suffer the same fate, if identified and caught. 'Peace be with you,' the risen Lord declared, not once but three times. It was much more than a conventional greeting on his lips in those circumstances. They would have recalled his earlier words, spoken not long before. 'Peace I leave with you; my peace I give you...'(14:27). Peace to frightened followers; peace to a doubting disciple caught in a crisis of faith; peace to us too when we are uncertain, insecure and frightened.

The Commissioning Christ

The risen Christ is the commissioning Christ. What we call 'The Great Commission' appears in all four gospels. The most familiar form is in Matthew 28:16-20. Here in John 20:19-23 we find the most neglected version, relegated to the margins of our consciousness according to Mortimer Arias. Short in words, deficient in details, it is yet breathtaking in its consequences. 'As the Father has sent me, I am sending you,' says Jesus to his disciples. 'And with that,' we are told, 'he breathed on them and said, "Receive the Holy Spirit".'

John Stott speaks of this as the most crucial form of the Great Commission for today, 'the most neglected because it is the most costly' (*Christian Mission in the Modern World*). Deliberately and precisely Jesus makes his own incarnational style of mission the model for ours. As Jesus was sent, so we are sent into the world. We are sent to suffer, to serve and to witness for Christ and his kingdom. It costs.

The Greek word for 'witness' is the word from which the

English word 'martyr' is derived. In the early church, believers often had to seal their witness with their blood. 'Martyrdom and mission belong together. Martyrdom is especially at home on the mission field' (quoted by David Bosch in *Transforming Mission*). That is true, we add, whether the mission takes place in Zambia or Ireland.

At its best, Christian mission is long-term, costly and carries risk. It is rooted firmly in Christ's life, death and resurrection, is enabled by the Spirit and is made relevant to each time and place. The Christian faith, unlike a potted plant, simply cannot be moved from one place and set down in another. If it is to take root in its new setting, the pot and packaging need to be broken. In other words, we need to learn how to distinguish between the gospel itself and its cultural expressions. This is just as necessary in the many sub-cultures of Ireland as in any other country in the world. That is one of our greatest challenges today.

The Liberating Christ
The risen Christ is the liberating Christ. The disciples were over-joyed when they saw the Lord (v. 20). The presence of the Lord and the power of the Spirit liberate. Jesus and the Holy Spirit free us from sin, from paralysing fear and from the bondage of an unforgiving heart (vv. 21-23). They free us for life, witness and service.

A huge statue, Christ the Redeemer, stands over the city of Rio de Janeiro with arms outstretched. On the slopes behind the statue is a large *favella*, a slum which is home to the poorest of the poor. To some it must seem that Christ has turned his back on the poor. 'Not so,' says a community worker in the area, 'he is leading us out of the *favella*.'

Our mission is to win people for Jesus Christ and to trans-form society. We are to pray and work for a world in which all are included in the feast of life. In Christ we see how costly it is to bring that world about. For us there are no 'no-go areas'. We follow where Christ leads. Our calling is to leave the safety of our Christian enclaves, 'to go unrecognised, to live without honour and to give ourselves in total sacrifice' (Rob Frost). As Mother Teresa said, we are to learn to 'love until it hurts'. Are we up to it? It is only possible by God's grace, through faith in Christ, empowered by the Holy Spirit.

Prayer:
Gather and scatter us, O Lord, according to your will.
Build us into one church with open doors and
large windows, which takes the whole world seriously.
As we follow Christ and witness to his kingdom
may we be ready to work and suffer
for those for whom he died. Amen.
(Eastern Europe, adapted)

The call to ministry

Peter Stephens

'*Come with me, and I will make you fishers of men.*' (Mark 1:17)
You are ordained into the church of Christ which stretches back
twenty centuries to our Lord himself who was present with his
people then and who is present with us now. Therefore I want to
direct you, not to our history but to the scriptures, to that moment
when our Lord first called the disciples in Mark 1:17 in the
words: 'Come with me, and I will make you fishers of men.' I
want you to see in these words that the ministry which you exercise is Christ's ministry and not yours.

First, it is rooted in the call of Christ, who says 'Come.'
The beginning of the Christian life, as of the Christian ministry,
is with Christ and not with you. Through the whole of scripture,
as we look at those who have dealings with God, we see that the
beginning lies, not with men and women in choosing God, but
with God choosing men and women. We see this dramatically in
the Old Testament in the call of the prophets, where Jeremiah
was set apart by God, even in the womb. It is the same when we
come to the life of Christ. It isn't as though the disciples decide
to follow him. It is rather that he calls them. He comes to where
Peter, James, John and Andrew are at work and he calls them to
follow him. The same is true of the other disciples who, like
them, were made apostles, for a ministry is given to them in that
original calling to follow him. This ministry was later confirmed
and empowered by the risen Lord.

What about the other disciples like Zacchaeus? Does not the
initiative lie with him when he climbed the tree because he was
so small? No, for the crucial moment in the story is when Jesus
says: 'Zacchaeus, come down, for I must come to your house

today.' That was the starting point: when the curiosity of Zacchaeus to hear this man was turned by the initiative of Christ into a call to discipleship.

Now turn the pages of the New Testament to Paul in Acts chapter 9. Paul was set against Christ, but he was halted in his tracks. However, that was not the end but rather an open-ended, mysterious beginning. He was sent, he did not know where, to hear a message of which he did not yet know. When he got there it was Ananias who brought the word of God to him. Moreover, Ananias did not go willingly, for Paul had been an enemy of Christ. But to Ananias was vouchsafed the call of Paul who was to be a chosen vessel of the Lord.

In each of these cases it was the initiative of God in Jesus Christ which called them to discipleship. Moreover, with Paul and the apostles, in the moment of their call to discipleship, there came a call also to apostleship and ministry.

There are two days in the year when I reflect on the ministry into which I have been ordained and read the whole of the ordination service. The first is 7 July, when I was ordained to the ministry of the church of Christ. The second is 18 November when I first responded to the call to the ministry. You might think that 18 November highlights rather my decision than God's choice. It doesn't, because I did not wish to become a minister. I had resisted the call. I went to university and had wanted to do three things: become a politician, a diplomat or a barrister. To my friends, some of those are more surprising than others. That was where my heart was set and I believed I could serve God as a lay person, perhaps as a local preacher as many do. It was not until my ambition was surrendered to God that I was able to hear the call of God to the ministry. On 18 November I commemorate that the call came to me and I was able to follow it with the whole of my life and not every part of my life except my job.

You must remember your call to ministry. You will go through dark days when you might wish you were not in the ministry. Sometimes it will be those in the church who will be the greatest trial to you. At those moments you will need to know that you are not in the ministry because of your family, or your friends, or your church, but because God in his mercy has called you.

Your ministry is rooted in the call of Christ.

Secondly, it is rooted in the commission of Christ. 'I will make you fishers of men.'
This may appear sexist, but some translate it even less helpfully as 'I will make you catch men.'

The ministry is not about your talents. That is not a comment on your ministerial training. You may be gifted academically or pastorally. You may be assiduous in discipline. You may even think you are God's gift to the church. Indeed, in a profound sense, you are God's gift to the church. You are God's gift, not because you are an outstanding intellectual or an exceptional administrator. No. Jesus says, 'I will make you fishers of men.' In other words, it is not that you have it in you to be fishers of men. Rather 'I will make you.' True prophets have always known that it is God who makes them effective, not their own ability. Jeremiah knew his inadequacy, but God said, 'I will put my words into your mouth.' Your prophetic ministry does not depend on your words but on the words God gives you.

Nor is your ministry about your experience, though it can be enriched by your experience. Some have an experience of the evangelical Christ which is a sense of the wonder of the love of God in Christ's death for you and a sense of amazement that you are a child of God. You believe that you are called to share that amazing good news with others. Some have an experience of the pentecostal Christ who by the Holy Spirit has freed you from inhibition in your life and witness and worship. It is this sense of liberty and life in the Spirit that has brought you to respond to the call. Some have an experience of the political Christ and have been moved by the need of people across the world. You have seen the poverty and injustice and you want to stand with Christ in the work of liberation.

You will bring your experience of Christ to your preaching. But it's not your experience that you preach. It is Christ whom you preach. The Christ you preach will not be simply the Christ of your experience, but rather the Christ of the church and of the New Testament. He is larger than any of our experiences of him. Your commission is rooted in him, not in your experience of him, not in your grasp of him or even in the way that he has grasped you. Your commission is rooted in the One who has made himself known to us and his church.

The ministry which you exercise is rooted in his commission. He is the centre and focus of it. If when you leave your circuit they simply say things like: 'He or she was a wonderful visitor, a fine preacher, a good administrator,' and so on, then perhaps your ministry has been rooted in yourself and in your gifts and not in him. When you leave, I hope they will remember him, and you in the remembering of him.

Thirdly, your ministry is rooted in the company of Christ.
Between the call and the commission are the words: 'Come with me'.

The company of Christ is first the company of his companions who become your companions. A companion is literally 'one with whom one eats bread'. You are not called to minister alone. You are called to serve within the church which is his company. The church will not be the company of the entirely sanctified any more than the church in the New Testament was. If you had been stationed in the Corinth church you would have complained that it was not a suitable place to which to send an inexperienced minister – a church where there was drunkenness, incest, arrogance, and almost every imaginable sin. You would not have seen this as an appropriate place for your holy ministry. But Paul was not so choosy.

If you had been called to the company of the apostles, no doubt you would have been rather sniffy about some of them. If you had been called from being a tax collector, scoundrel that you were, you would not have expected to be with Simon the zealot, fiery nationalist that he was. Political difference exists within the church as it did in the company of the apostles. If you want a community that exactly reflects your own remarkable character then you must found a band of admirers and set up on your own. But if you are to be a minister in the church of Christ, you will accept those Christ has given you. Some will be further on the way than you are. Some will not be far at all on the way. Some will meet you going in the opposite direction! They are God's gift to you and you are God's gift to them. So the company of Christ means his companions who are also your companions.

More intimately, however, the company of Christ means the company of our Lord himself. Your life is to be rooted in his company. You will lead people in prayer. It is too easy to stand in the pulpit leading others in prayer, but neglect to pray in your room. You will preach the word of God, teaching others. It is too easy to read the word of God to preach to others, but not to read it in order to be shaped by it in your own life. Some of the promises we make at ordination are concerned to see that our lives and our ministry are rooted in the company of Christ. Day by day we need to live in that personal discipline of prayer and the study of his word, in the fellowship of Christian people, in the colleagueship of the ministry in which you build each other up, and in the worship of the church.

Your ministry is rooted in Christ: in his call to you, 'Come', to which you have responded; in his commission to you, 'I will make you fishers of men' when he gives the Holy Spirit to equip you, and others, with the necessary gifts; in his company, 'Come with me', when he unites you with himself and others.

I was once at a promenade concert at the Royal Albert Hall, with Sir Adrian Boult conducting Beethoven's *Pastoral Symphony*. At the end of the performance, the audience cheered. Sir Adrian Boult did not, like some footballer who had just scored a goal, punch the air with his fist for the acclaim of the crowds. Instead he took up the score of Beethoven's music. The applause was for Beethoven, not for Boult.

The greatest thing that can be said of your ministry is that

you led people to Christ and that in your life, now and then, they
caught a glimpse of the Christ whom you serve.

Prayer:
Loving God our Father, we give you thanks that in Jesus Christ
you have called us to follow you. We pray that we may hear that
call anew and be renewed in our own discipleship. May we be
those who – with our prayers and words of encouragement –
support and sustain those whom you called to the sacred ministry of Christ in his church.

Motivation for ministry

Cecil Newell

'Be not weary in well-doing' (Galatians 6:9)
There is an expression in the language of the Shona people of
Zimbabwe, *'Musanete mangwana!'* It literally means, 'Do not grow
tired to-morrow' and is a way of saying as a word of thanks –
'Carry on the good work you have been doing.'

It is a word we all need to hear, for it is so easy in Christian
service, when it becomes difficult and costly, to grow tired and
give up. Paul knew this well and encouraged the Galatian
Christians not to become weary in well doing.

There are three things that Christians need to remember if
they are to continue to toil without tiring and to fight the good
fight without flagging. They need to remember that however
difficult their service may be, they are doing a great work, discharging a great debt and drawing on great strength.

In Christian service we are doing a great work
What keeps us going is a sense of the importance of the task in
which we are involved.

When Nehemiah was engaged in supervising the rebuilding
of the walls of Jerusalem, he faced not only the physical difficulty
of the task, but also strong opposition from neighbours who
didn't want the Jews to become a strong people again in a well-
defended city. However, when Sanballat and Geshem invited
Nehemiah to come down for a meeting with them in the Valley
of Ono, planning to do him mischief and remove him from his
wall-building, his firm reply was, 'I am doing a great work and
cannot come down.'

When Jesus hung on the cross, the bystanders mocked him

and said, 'If you are the Son of God, save yourself and come down from the cross!' He could have come down, but instead he remained on the cross that he might win the salvation of mankind. Like Nehemiah, he could have said, 'I am doing a great work and cannot come down.'

In Christian service we are doing a great work, a work of eternal importance, seeking the salvation and eternal good of people, each one of whom Jesus saw as of greater value than the whole world.

Paul carried the gospel into the world of his day because he had learned from Jesus the eternal value of each human life, whether Jew or Gentile, male or female, bond or free. He realised how much people mattered and was encouraged to continue ministering to others, in spite of the cost, because he saw each individual as 'the brother for whom Christ died'.

What a difference it makes when we see people, not just as 'others' but as 'brothers'! A lady was drawing the curtains one evening at dusk and saw the outline of two people crossing the road and being struck by a car. She didn't want to become involved, so she hurried into her kitchen and busied herself preparing the evening meal. Later that evening there was a knock at the door. A policeman had called with the sad news that her parents had both been killed in a car accident down the street, evidently on their way to visit her. You can guess the reaction! How different her response would have been at the sight of the accident if she had realised that the victims were her own kith and kin!

How different our attitude would be to those we may find it difficult to go on serving, if we were more aware of them as our brothers and sisters! We need also to remember that those we are called to serve are people for whom Christ died. This is why we should place such high value on them.

Sometimes people have brought along to an Antique Road Show an old painting which has been lying in the dust of an attic for years and have been surprised to be told by an expert that the picture would fetch tens of thousands of pounds in an auction.

The value of their picture was revealed by being told what someone would pay for it. The Christian should always remember how valuable is a human soul in the light of what Jesus was prepared to pay in his sacrifice on the cross to save it.

In Christian service we are discharging a great debt
When Jesus sent out the twelve to preach and heal, he added words that form one of the strongest reasons for becoming involved in a life of service. He said, 'Freely you have received, freely give.' From the first breath we have breathed we have received blessing upon blessing, physically and spiritually, beyond all numbering. We have received from God the supreme and unspeakable gift of his Son and through him the gift of eternal life.

How moved and challenged the first disciples must have been when, on the first Easter evening, Jesus appeared to them and showed them his hands and his side, proof not only that he was indeed Jesus risen from the dead, but the sign of his gracious sacrifice for their redemption. Then, when he said to them, 'As the Father has sent me, I am sending you,' they knew that they couldn't refuse the commission of one who had suffered so much for them.

When Paul urged the Christians at Rome to present their bodies as a living sacrifice in God's service, he said that he was beseeching them to do this 'by the mercies of God'. In their service they were discharging a great debt.

Paul's missionary journeys across the world of his day have been described as 'the tracks of a bleeding hare across the snow'. He suffered stoning and beating, hunger and thirst, shipwreck and imprisonment and so much hardship. If you had spoken to him as he gathered himself up and wiped the blood from his face and continued on his way to proclaim Christ, and asked him why he did it, he would have replied, 'The love of Christ constrains me.' He was discharging a great debt.

Dr Mason, a missionary in Burma, once asked a local man if he would be willing to go to a certain village and carry the gospel there. It was a dangerous mission, among the Bgais. The missionary offered him the payment of four rupees a month. Shupau, the man he asked to take on this mission, shook his head and replied, 'No, teacher, I couldn't go there for four rupees a month; but I could go for Christ.' He went to the difficult area and his work was greatly blessed, and as a result of his faithful ministry there a thousand converts were baptised and forty churches were established. He was able to do this work because he realised in doing it that he was discharging a great debt.

Whatever work we undertake in Christian service we should never give up because it becomes difficult, unless we feel that we can comfortably place our resignation into the hands of Jesus that were wounded for us.

In Christian service we are drawing on great strength
Jesus warned those whom he called to become his followers that they would face many difficulties and hardships in his service. They would have to deny themselves and take up their cross. However, he assured them that all the strength they would need for their service would be available. When he commissioned them to 'go' into all the world and proclaim the good news of the gospel, he added, 'Lo I am with you always, even unto the end of the world.' When he commissioned them to be his witnesses (and this included witnessing through suffering) he promised them that they would receive power.

It is all too easy to be discouraged in Christian service by fearing that we won't be able to bear the cross and that we won't be successful in the task we undertake in his service. Jesus promises that we shall be given the strength both to endure and to succeed.

When God called Joshua to succeed Moses in leading the Israelites to the promised land, he knew that Joshua's heart was filled with misgivings and fears. So he encouraged him to go forward assured of his presence and his power by saying, 'As I was with Moses, so shall I be with you. I will not fail you nor forsake you. Be strong and of a good courage. … Be strong and of a good courage ... Be strong and of a good courage; don't be afraid nor dismayed, for the Lord your God is with you, wherever you go.' Three times God tells Joshua to 'be strong' and assures him of the enabling strength of his presence with him.

We have the promise, 'They who wait upon the Lord shall renew their strength. They shall mount up with wings as eagles. They shall run without wearying and walk without fainting.'

Isaac Watts expresses this truth in the words of one of his hymns:

True, 'tis a strait and thorny road and mortal spirits tire and faint;

But they forget the mighty God, that feeds the strength of every saint.

God's strength not only enables us to endure, but it enables us to achieve. In his letter to the Galatians, where Paul deals with this danger of losing heart, he writes, 'Be not weary in well-doing, for in due season you shall reap your reward, if you faint not.'

These are words which John Wesley quoted in the last letter he wrote, towards the end of his earthly life. It was written to William Wilberforce, who at the time was engaged in an uphill struggle to achieve the abolition of slavery. In the letter Wesley writes, 'Unless God has raised you up for this very thing, you will be worn out by the opposition of men and devils; but, if God be for you, who can be against you? Are all of them together stronger than God? Oh be not weary in well-doing! Go in the name of God and in the power of his might, till the vilest slavery that ever saw the light of day shall vanish before it.'

With God all things are possible and by his almighty strength Christians can overcome and win a glorious victory and reap a great harvest. Jesus shall reign! We do not yet see all things put under his feet, but we see him crowned and all his foes will one day be overcome. The gates of hell cannot stand against the power of Christ at work through his Holy Spirit in his church.

In an old film entitled *I'd climb the highest mountain* there is a part where an old doctor was battling against a serious epidemic and reached a point of despair, which he shared with the young preacher by saying, 'I'm licked.' When the preacher responded by saying that he only felt licked because he was tired (and this can so often be the case), the doctor added, 'No. I feel tired because I'm licked.'

It is all too easy to feel tired and weary because we fear that we aren't going to succeed. We can renew our ebbing strength by remembering that in God's strength we are guaranteed a victory.

Archbishop Desmond Tutu, who was engaged in a long battle against the South African policy and practice of apartheid, has told of how during debate with the advocates of apartheid, he would often smile and say, 'Why don't you join the winning side?' He knew that God would triumph and everything that opposed the will of God was doomed ultimately to perish.

What encouragement there is in the words in Psalm 126: 'They who go forth weeping, bearing precious seed, shall doubtless come again with rejoicing, bringing their sheaves with them.' Weeping will give way to rejoicing and the handfuls of seed will become armfuls of sheaves.

The power that raised Jesus from the dead is available to all who engage in his service and can cause us always to triumph. So keep on keeping on. *Musanete mangwana!* Do not grow tired tomorrow! Well-doing is worth doing, ought to be done and can be done, in the power of Christ.

Prayer:
O Father, shake me out of my circles.
Let me have a deathless hope of an infinite plan,
infinitely unfolding. Amen.
E Stanley Jones

God's own people

Gearoid O'Sullivan CM

1 Peter 1:18-21:
'You know well that it was nothing of passing value,
like silver or gold, that bought your freedom
from the futility of your traditional ways.
You were set free by Christ's precious blood,
blood like that of a lamb without mark or blemish.
He was predestined before the foundation of the world,
but in this last period of time he has
been revealed for your sake.
Through him you have come to trust in God
Who raised him from the dead and gave him glory,
and so your faith and hope are fixed
on God.'

Dear new graduates, diplomats, family and friends ... just a few words on this benchmark day in your lives.

The passage from the First Letter of Peter proclaims a *people* – God's people – a people that has become God's own possession. The challenge here for each of you is to *be* a people. Not simply because God has called you to be such. The human society you are entering, summons you, needs you desperately, precisely as a *people*.

Let me explain. Sociologists have been describing a disturbing development, a frightening phenomenon. They see society moving away from older character ideals, away from religious man or woman – away from political man or woman. Both these ideals were oriented to the public world – the community – the *common good*, the *other*.

But when the central institution in our society is no longer religion or the political order but the *economy* – the ideal is now economic man or woman – man or woman in pursuit of private self-interest.

Why challenge you new graduates with this? Because this new ideal finds its strength in the younger generations. The dominant theme researchers find in you economic man or woman is freedom, autonomy, personal fulfilment; your sole responsibility is to yourself; in the end you are *alone.*

Is there any solution to this? Yes, there is. We are called to be the people of God, what Saint Paul calls the *Body* of *Christ.*

A non-religious sociologist suggests: 'Only the church as a type of Christian social organisation can effectively combat the radical individualism and managerial manipulation of modern society.' The church, as the Body of Christ, can remind us that we will survive only in so far as we *care* for one another. As Christians and as citizens we might just possibly recover an idea of the common good, of that which is *good* in itself and not just the good of private desire.

As a people – as a living body where if I am hurt, you weep; if I rejoice, you laugh; if I die, you are diminished. The tragedy is, sympathetic scholars tell us, the church body has been more conditioned by the culture than an influence upon it.

How ready are *you* to resist the culture? In all professions there are already individuals who do. But Don Quixotes will not change the culture. The culture will change, only if educated men and women in massive numbers carry their Christianity into the market place and financial institutions, into law courts and genetic laboratories, conscious of their solidarity with every man, woman and child 'redeemed not with silver and gold but with the precious blood of Christ' (1 Pet 1:18-19).

There is no need to fashion a Christian economics but to make economic man or woman serve the human person. Paradoxically, only thus will your profession be your servant, not you its slave.

Prayer:
Hush our world's seductive voices
tempting us to stand alone;
save us, then from siren noises
calling us to trust our own.
For those snared by earthly treasure,
lured by false security,
Jesus, true and only measure,
spring the trap to set folk free.
Leith Fisher from Common Ground

Sent to serve

Kwesi Dickson

Jesus said to them, 'Peace be with you.
As the Father has sent me, so I send you.'
When he had said this, he breathed on them and said to them,
'Receive the Holy Spirit.' *(John 20:21-22)*

To study the New Testament closely is to end up with a fascinating picture of the twelve disciples who had responded to Jesus' call to follow him. A more ordinary bunch of people one could hardly find. Peter, whose brother was Andrew, was a fisherman. His partners were James and John (Lk 5:10), sons of Zebedee, whose mother had wanted Jesus to give her boys preferential treatment (Mt 20:20f). Matthew was a tax collector, one of that class of people who collaborated with the Roman government, and who were despised by the people for their habit of enriching themselves by demanding more money than they should and pocketing the excess. Simon the Cananaean, and perhaps also Judas Iscariot, belonged to the group of people known as the Zealots whose desire was to use force against their Roman masters.

They were so ordinary that they were not above speaking almost rudely to Jesus, as when they said to him as he lay asleep in the boat which was being roughly tossed about on the lake in rough weather: 'Teacher, do you not care that we are perishing?' (Mk 4:38). There was the other occasion when Jesus had asked the disciples to give the five thousand people who were with them in a deserted place something to eat. Their reaction had been: 'Are we to go and buy two hundred denarii worth of bread, and give it to them to eat?' (Mk 6:37). What they were in effect saying was: 'You should know better, master: Where do we find a labourer's twenty days' wages to provide bread for this lot?'

Writing after Mark, Matthew and Luke endeavour to tone down the roughness of the disciples' language. There is no reason to doubt, however, that those reactions and remarks found in Mark truly represented the disciples as they were – so much under the control of their human wisdom and emotions. They sometimes failed to understand Jesus' teaching, as when just before the ascension they asked him, 'Lord, is this the time when you will restore the kingdom to Israel?' (Acts 1:6). That the significance of much of what Jesus had said about the kingdom had been missed by the disciples is clear. Their question shows that they were expecting the restoration of a political kingdom, like that of King David under whom Israel's political star had shone very brightly indeed. Jesus' response seeks to draw his disciples' attention away from a political kingdom to the renewal of Israel's vocation to evangelise the world. The disciples were indeed ordinary, unsophisticated people, slow to understand, and even uncertain as to whether or not the cross was inevitable (Mt 16:13f).

But before we begin to write off those disciples, who shared so many experiences with Jesus, as being undeserving of Jesus' company and attention, we must realise that throughout the history of the church many so-called believers have often been plagued by doubts in the face of life's many uncertainties, particularly as they affect our humanity. Doubts about the goodness of God can sometimes arise in situations of suffering – and there have been mind-boggling atrocities committed in Africa. Furthermore, we often betray Christ ourselves, by our lack of faith and compassion, or by our desire for worldly recognition, or by our inability and unwillingness to forgive. The truth of the matter is that we have little cause to pat ourselves on the back and claim to have more understanding and commitment than those twelve disciples of Jesus.

But let us go to the story of the disciples as it has to do with the death and resurrection of Christ and out of which our text comes. When Jesus was arrested, sentenced to death and crucified, the disciples were assailed by doubt and fear. They doubted because it must have been difficult for them to understand how one who claimed to be Son of God should come to such an end. They feared, evidently believing that they themselves, as Jesus' followers, might suffer the same fate. According to John's gospel, the disciples shut the doors of the room in which they were – they were not taking any chances. It must also have been a time of introspection, wondering about this man Jesus whom they had accompanied. One can imagine the impetuous Peter wondering whether he had been wise to leave off his trade in order to follow Jesus. It was in these circumstances that 'Jesus came and stood among them and said to them, "Peace be with you".'

The word 'peace' must have startled the disciples. While it was an ordinary word of greeting, much as one would say 'Good morning', those who translated the Old Testament into the Greek language gave the word 'shalom' several meanings. They saw it as meaning not only peace but also health and salvation. That the word for greeting should have such a rich significance should not surprise the African. When two Africans greet each other, it is not merely a matter of saying 'Good morning'. The greeting invariably goes on to ask about the other's personal and family circumstances. Indeed, greeting can be a prolonged affair which involves inquiries regarding health and well-being of the family. I am inclined to think that in that word 'peace', Jesus meant much more than an ordinary greeting. The conventional term was being given added significance. They must have heard in that word Jesus saying to them: 'Let there be peace in your hearts and consciences. I still trust you, no matter how unfaithful and insensitive you may have been.'

That is the scandal of Christianity – that Jesus should deem us righteous who fail to worship him in our hearts and live his teaching. The very coming of the Christian faith is a story which has much significance in this connection. At a time when the military might of Rome was earning her victory after victory, a faith was born which taught that it was by patient love and even suffering that the kingdom of God would be established. Did

Jesus not wash his disciples' feet when the world expects the servant to attend to the needs of the master? Did he not take the
side of the woman caught in adultery – a religious teacher ap-
parently condoning immorality? Did he not highly commend
the poor woman who put two copper coins in the offertory
when someone else might only have noticed the rich men in
their finery? The parable of the Prodigal Son features a father
who acted the way many a father would not act. Seeing his way-
ward son approaching the house he went outside to meet him.
Some other father would have stayed put and with disdain
watched the ungrateful son step timidly inside the house and
grovel before him.

There was more for the disciples to learn from the risen
Christ. Having wished them well, Jesus went on to say to them
'As the Father has sent me so I send you.' Was it not enough for
Jesus to have expressed confidence in the disciples? Did he have
to send them since they had in many ways failed him? Was he
not taking chances sending them? One can almost see the disciples looking furtively at one another, the same thought having
occurred to each of them: 'Is he serious, after all that we have
been and done?' Evidently, though Jesus continued to love and
care about them, he had no desire to make them feel smug.
God's work must be done and the disciples must go out to
preach. Earlier in the course of his ministry Jesus had sent out
the Twelve and the Seventy to preach, teach and heal (Lk 9:1;
10:1). By sending the disciples after expressing his confidence in
them, he was reminding them that the essence of his mission lay
in proclaiming God's message of salvation. Do we not all need
to be reminded daily about this?

One of the insidious temptations facing ministers of religion
is for them to see themselves simply as managers of an establishment who write reports, and sermons and chair meetings.
Indeed, ministers can become so engrossed in their managerial
role that it is with much reluctance that they delegate responsibility to others. It is sobering to realise that the minister is vulnerable. So much hangs on his or her shoulders that there may

be much reluctance to admit to, or little awareness of, having lost the urge that led one into the ministry.

The minister's central role is to go and preach the gospel, demonstrating that God cares for people in their spiritual as well as material circumstances. We cease to be disciples if we fail to get out and proclaim the message of salvation. As soon as those disciples found themselves back in the fold of Christ's followers, they were reminded that their being disciples lay in their serving Christ in the world.

Fortunately, to those whom God in Christ sends, he gives the power to do his will. According to our text, Jesus 'breathed on them, and said to them, "Receive the Holy Spirit".' One cannot help recalling Genesis 2:7 which reads: '(the Lord God) breathed into (the man's) nostrils the breath of life and the man became a living being.' Thus Jesus gave the disciples the saving breath of the new life which would imbue them with the power to do as directed by him.

But perhaps the reader of the New Testament will be puzzled by this reference to the Holy Spirit in connection with Easter Day. In The Acts of the Apostles we read that the Holy Spirit came upon the believers following Jesus' ascension. We seem, then, to have two unreconciled accounts of when the Spirit was given. There is really no contradiction, however. There is no reason to doubt that there was a bestowal of the Spirit at Easter; after that, there must have been a time of waiting when the Spirit worked among the apostles, until the Day of Pentecost when there was that great release of power which gave the apostles new life. Those disciples who had shut themselves up in a room following Jesus' death became leaders who fearlessly preached the message of salvation.

It surely must be true that the Spirit works continually in the hearts of those who believe in God. There is a tendency to associate the working of the Spirit only with powerful, external phenomena, like the 'great wind, so strong that it was splitting mountains and breaking rocks in pieces', or like the earthquake or the fire (1 Kings 19:11-13) and we can forget that the Holy Spirit can also be in 'a sound of sheer silence' (1 Kings 19:12). According to the scriptures the Spirit is ever present, like the wind which 'blows where it chooses, and you hear the sound of it, but you do not know where it comes from or where it goes' (Jn 3:8).

By breathing on the disciples and saying to them, 'Receive the Holy Spirit', Jesus, the giver of life, strengthens them for the task which they are to perform in the world: preaching, teaching and healing.

This text says a great deal to me as a minister of religion, especially at this time when the world seems to have little desire for peace and justice. The twentieth century has been the most violent and brutish in history. In the last decade or so there has been much fighting in various parts of Africa. Many young lives have been lost, and young boys, hardly in their teens, have been bearing arms. Life has become unbearable for many, especially the women who bear so much responsibility in African society. Because of such evils as ethnic cleansing, Africa has produced millions of refugees, men and women and children who have crossed national borders in search of a better life for themselves. This has made many in Africa more conscious than ever of the need for national reconciliation. There is little doubt that reconciliation is needed but how is it to be achieved? Reconciliation cannot come about through legislation; it cannot be achieved simply because people express a desire for it; goodwill is not enough to ensure reconciliation. To be involved in reconciliation one has first to be reconciled in oneself. That is where reconciliation begins – in the individual's heart. The individual must have the peace of God for reconciliation to take place. At this time, more than ever, the world needs the peace of God and the in-breathing of the Spirit.

All of us are called by God to serve him and we need to be aware that it is not by our wisdom that reconciliation and justice will come to prevail in society. Ordinary eloquence is insufficient for the task of preaching Christ. The eloquence needed is the type that enables one's audience to hear Christ himself speaking. The human speaker must not be at the centre of the message – that position belongs to Christ and Christ alone. We may set much store by an ordination certificate, but in truth it is the Spirit which certifies that one is indeed in the ministry of Christ's church.

Those who seek to serve God have access to the power that was demonstrated nowhere more strikingly than on the cross.

Prayer:

Glory be to you, O Lord our God, that in your Son Jesus Christ you have given us the pioneer and perfecter of our faith. Give us the grace to know that we cannot lead unless he leads us; we cannot preach his word unless he speaks his word through us; and we cannot reconcile unless he reconciles us to himself. And let us be led by that love which took him to the Cross to serve you and your people. In his name we pray. Amen.

To a newly ordained presbyter

Bruce B Swapp

'I am among you as one who serves.' Luke 22:27

Congratulations. You have been ordained to the office and work of a presbyter and we rejoice with you.

We rejoice with you because your ordination means that there is one more servant dedicated to this ministry of the church. Your ordination means that there is one more Christian presbyter and pastor, who has publicly and without ambiguity, declared full commitment to this ministry of Christ and the church.

We rejoice, because with that commitment you have declared that you will preach with conviction, evangelise with enthusiasm and faithfully administer the holy sacraments in the name of the Father, the Son and the Holy Spirit.

We rejoice because we have another pastor committed to be a faithful representative of the Chief Shepherd. Our members, therefore, have another minister who is prepared to be a shepherd to the people; who is dedicated to uphold the weak, to heal the sick, to bind up the broken and to bring back the outcasts and those who are lost.

We rejoice because the church has another administrator, who is willing in Christ's name to be merciful without being slack and to administer the discipline of the church with grace and compassion.

For this great and demanding work, we have by the imposition of hands reaffirmed the presence of the Holy Spirit in your life, praying that the Spirit will guide you in the fulfilment of your ministry of word and sacraments.

In addition, recognising that all authority in heaven and on earth has been given to our Lord, our Saviour and Master, we have sought to convey to you this authority derived from the same Lord by giving you a bible, the word of God, as a symbol and token of that authority.

Hence our words: 'Take this (Bible) as your authority as you fulfil the office of a presbyter and pastor in the church of Christ.'

Your authority comes from Christ the Head of the church and, therefore, when humbly accepted and faithfully discharged it is not circumscribed by the boundaries of the MCCA. You are a minister in the church of Christ, and the bible that we have given you symbolises this extension of your ministry, your potential influence and your derived authority.

But you have also acknowledged that your commitment to service has been made within a particular fellowship, that is, within that section of the church that was raised up to spread scriptural holiness throughout the land and to reform the nation. Your lineage and linkage are with the people called Methodists and specifically with the Methodist Church in the Caribbean and the Americas.

You have been ordained a presbyter in the Church Universal for it is by the one Holy Spirit of God our Father that you have been ordained to the ministry of the one Lord who is our Saviour Jesus Christ.

However, you have also declared your belief that you have been called to be a minister in the Methodist Church in the Caribbean and the Americas and it is through this church within the Body of Christ that your call was expressed, recognised, tested and confirmed. It is through this church that you have pledged to exercise your sacred ministry.

That is why, in addition to your being ordained by us, you have also been received by our Conference as a minister in full Connexion with the MCCA. Thereby the MCCA acknowledges you as a minister within its ranks and all that that means for your appointment in and your support by the church.

Consequently, you have declared your willingness to submit yourself to the discipline of the MCCA which must necessarily be administered by fellow ministers who themselves would have been appointed and authorised to do so in the various offices of the church.

You see then, the importance of recognising the source of our authority and so to speak, the line of authority in the church. Even more important in my opinion, is the recognition of the nature of this authority given to you, what it is and what it is not.

Jesus told his disciples: 'You know that the rulers of the gentiles lord it over them; and their great ones are tyrants over them. It will not be so among you; but whoever wishes to be great among you must be your servant, and whoever wishes to be first among you must be your slave; just as the Son of Man came not to be served but to serve and to give his life a ransom for many' (Mt 20:25-28).

This passage from Matthew, with its parallel in Luke, is simple, clear and straightforward. Your authority makes you a servant not a despot. Your authority is for service and not for domination. I read somewhere that 'the most noble use of authority is for serving others'. As Jesus himself said, 'I am among you as one who serves' (Lk 22:27).

Service is the mark of our authority as presbyters. Sometimes we give the impression that our authority is to do as we please and sometimes we may even declare and insist upon our right to exercise power. Unfortunately, within the context of our church meetings, such impressions and declarations are hardly challenged. That does not mean that they are not discussed vigorously outside of meetings, but it is unfortunate that so many of our congregational and circuit leaders allow us as ministers to have our own way, which we are seeing as the competent exercise of our authority

I pray that the authority vested in you will always be used for the fulfilment of your ministry.

You have authority to preach. Do not take that responsibility lightly. Sometimes our preaching becomes a mere multiplication of words, because we have forgotten the source of our derived authority. Sometimes our preaching is nothing more than denunciation, which is often the result of lack of preparation compounded by failure to be persistent in our reading and to meditate often on the message of the Bible.

You have authority to preach. With God's help you will preach with authority.

You have authority to comfort and sustain those committed to your care. You will sometimes feel inadequate and unequal to the task but, with prayer, God has his way of over-ruling our feelings.

Only God knows where at some critical times we get the energy, the wisdom and the words to be of help. Only God knows, because he is the source of our authority.

We cannot comfort and sustain by keeping our distance. We cannot comfort and sustain when we fail to keep in touch with our members. We cannot comfort and sustain when we so alienate others that they do not want to approach us.

You have authority to comfort and sustain those committed to your care. You will pray for them. Be not numbered with those that are described as hirelings.

You have authority to offer leadership to your congregations and community. People will look to you for guidance and direction. You will be called upon to administer discipline, to make decisions, and to speak up and to speak out.

You have authority to offer leadership, without becoming a despot, which is always possible if as a presbyter you forget the source of your derived authority.

God has called you and we are confident that he has bestowed the gifts of the spirit upon you, and that the grace and the fruit will indicate to the world that you were indeed chosen and called by God for this work.

We thank God for you and we commend you to his care and direction. We will continue to pray for you. May all things work together for good in your life as you seek to serve your Lord with faithfulness and, when the time comes that your derived authority is returned to the God who gave it, may your reward for faithful service endure throughout eternity.

To God be the glory now and for evermore.

Prayer:

Almighty God, you have given the will,
give also the strength to do your work
to the honour and glory of your name,
through Jesus Christ our Lord. Amen.

Models for mission

Ken Todd

'The Word became flesh and pitched his tent among us.' John 1:14
The opening verses of John's gospel are like a huge painting with
eternity and heaven as the background, linked with time and
earth in the foreground, and where the figure of Christ is at the
centre ground holding it all together. John the Baptist is there
also, but smaller and in the shadow of Christ. We view the painting and are awe-struck by the simplicity that belies its depth.

These verses have also been compared to an overture to an
enthralling symphony. Here again it is Christ who is the theme
music running through the whole piece, linking the motifs of
light, life, truth and glory. 'He brings light and at the same time
he is Light; he gives life and he is Life; he preaches truth and he
is Truth; he brings the word and he is the Word' (Geoffrey
Stone). We listen to the music and are moved from self-absorp-
tion to self-awareness and from contemplation to action.

By contrast, the opening words of an article in a special edi-
tion of a computer magazine for the year 2000 focuses on
Microsoft Word programmes and its founder: 'They say that in
the beginning was the Word. If that's true, then the reality is that
in the beginning was Bill Gates, and he begat Word. They must
have left that bit out of the Bible. But now just about everyone
uses Word.' The article then goes on to give '20 ways to get as
close to perfection as you ever will.'

John's gospel declares that perfection of Word is Jesus Christ
and in John 1:1-18 he suggests some templates for mission so
that we can publish the message to all the world.

God cares enough to communicate ('in the beginning was the word'. v 1).
How can we fathom what W. Temple called 'the unsearchable
abyss of Deity?' Reason, great gift that it is, is unable to reach
God so he communicates verbally and personally. God says: 'I
am giving you my Word, you can rely on me.' God speaks his
mind specially and savingly in scripture and in Christ. The Bible
is our supreme authority for faith and conduct and it is Christ
the living Word who makes sense of the Bible. Christ is the cen-
tre-ground of the biblical picture as he is the theme music of the
biblical symphony. 'Jesus not only brings revelation, but in his
person is revelation,' says Oscar Cullman. John Stott helpfully
notes that we speak of Alexander the Great, Herod the Great,
Napoleon the Great, but never Jesus the Great for he is Jesus the
Only.

In our visual and dramatic age, words are important as they
convey truth and the words of scripture are the most important
of all. It is by hearing the word that we come to Christ. It is by
obeying the word that we follow Christ. It is by spreading the
word that we win the world for Christ. The world needs to hear
the voice of its Maker because it so easily forgets. This means
that Christians will treasure and teach the gospel and will not
tamper with it to bring it onto line with worldly philosophies
which cannot save. We are in the communication business.

We will be gossips of the gospel. John the Baptiser came to be a
witness (v 7). Many Christians feel awkward about witnessing
and even the very word can be a turn-off. But we all can offer to
pray for someone or invite them to a gospel opportunity. People
often look for a saving word. Sometimes after a conversation we
hear people complain: '… and I never heard a word of thanks (or
encouragement, or apology) …' In a similar way the world is
waiting for a word from God. God has given the word. Too
many can still say '… and I never heard a word …' Sometimes
they never hear the word because they have never seen it in
action. Compassion can often open people's hearts where words
do not. God has bridged this credibility gap. John's prologue to
his gospel may be about the 'Word' but it is full of verbs and

actions as well as ideas. Donald English used to say: 'What God wants is not better salespersons but better samples.' Actions speak louder than words and both are needed. In Christ, the glory (awesome presence) of God was shown. Christians humbly desire always to give God the glory.

A little girl who was dependent on special care was travelling alone on a plane. A preacher sat beside her. She asked him 'Do you smoke?' 'No, I don't' he replied. She said, 'That's good, my mummy told me it's a good thing not to smoke.' Then after a few moments she persisted: 'Would you please ask the gentleman beside you if he smokes?' Slightly embarrassed he asked the passenger beside him and was assured that he didn't smoke either. The next question was: 'Do you love Jesus?' The preacher replied 'Yes, as a matter of fact I do'. The girl replied 'That's good. My mummy told me it is a good thing to love Jesus.' Then after a few moments she said 'Would you ask the gentleman beside you if he loves Jesus?' The preacher protested but to no avail so, with more embarrassment, he apologetically asked the stranger 'Do you love Jesus?' The stranger responded 'Well, as a matter of fact it is a question I have been thinking about for some time now and I was looking for someone to talk to about it.'

The Christian calling is to broadcast the precious gospel to all. Stanley Jones said, 'What is not worth exporting is not worth keeping.' Secular society, where God is missing but not missed, can never satisfy the aspirations of the human heart. God speaks, and we who have heard will want to tell the world like one beggar telling another where bread can be found.

We will be preachers of the gospel. A seminary professor once said, 'As preaching goes, so goes the church.' It is said that God had only one son and he was a preacher. Martin Luther spoke of the Bible preached as 'the cradle for Christ'. Many obituaries and more jokes have been written about preaching, like the enthusiast who received the uncertain advice: 'at the end of your sermon, those who do not arrive inspired will awake refreshed!' Yet people look for a word from the Lord from a messenger of the Lord in a face to face encounter, and what Paul called 'the foolishness of preaching' is 'the power of God unto salvation.' We must not undervalue preaching. It is said that Sermonettes make Christianettes, filleted Christians who have no backbone. We need evangelical preachers who are anointed by the Holy Spirit to expound the scriptures rather than their own fallible opinions, and we need prophetic preachers who relate the scriptures to right living today. Karl Barth spoke of preaching with a newspaper in one hand and the Bible in the other. Donald English spoke about the preacher having one foot in the scriptures and one foot in the world and taking the strain between the two. The evangelical preacher who proclaims Christ as Saviour and Lord, and the ethical preacher who proclaims Christ as teacher and example, have been compared to two wings on a bird, two oars in a boat, two hands on a clock, we need both.

The Reformation through Luther re-emphasised the scriptures as the central means of grace in the church. Today, in both Catholic and Reformed traditions, there is a greater sense of balance between the word and sacraments and between the verbal and the visual. Declaring the word of the Lord will, however, be always central to the church's worship. John Wesley called himself 'a man of one book' though he was widely read. Billy Graham when preaching used the phrase 'The Bible says.' John Stott when preaching holds a small Bible in his hands. We know that our Christian life stands or falls according to our obedience to holy scripture. The life-giving word of God is powerful (Heb 4:12). The source and the message remain unchanged while our methods of communication will vary. Demosthenes said the three requisites for oratory were, 'delivery, delivery, delivery'. The church needs preachers who delivery the goods.

Telling the story, is a model for mission.

God cares enough to come to us 'The word became flesh' (v 14).
C. S. Lewis called it 'The grand miracle' when God became human. God himself crossed the great divide in order to save the world. 'Being's source begins to be and God himself is born' (C. Wesley). The eternal entered time and awesomely became vul-

nerable to pain, temptation and death. This was more than a visitation, it was an incarnation. God really became human flesh with all its fullness and vulnerability. This is unique in world religions. If God crossed such an unthinkable barrier, Christians too will reach out to the lost, the least and the last.

Cross-border Christians

Too often we are borderline Christians when God indicates that he is calling us to be cross-border Christians. Trans-cultural missionaries are called and sent to remind the world that salvation comes from outside of ourselves and that the gospel has universal appeal. Part of the celebrations to welcome the new millennium in the cities of Dublin and Cork which have rivers flowing through them, included 'a lighting of the bridges' ceremony. At Bethlehem a star-lit bridge was built between heaven and earth. Christians are called to be lamp-lit bridges between the church and the world.

Lesley Johnston was a hairdresser who was converted to Christ and heard the call of Christ to share the gospel with new-age travellers living on the mountainous Celtic fringes of Ireland. For five years she has been living in rough conditions in a wooden house on a wind-swept mountain among people who have dropped out of the pressures of the rat race of modern society. This little lady, who used to be so particular about her appearance and hygiene, has embraced a lifestyle and a people that one time would have repulsed her. The reason is that God called her, filled her with his compassion and gave her the grace and grit of the Holy Spirit. Like Gladys Alyward, the little children love her and are now being taught in school and are learning to love Jesus. Lesley is a demonstration of love incarnate and of words becoming flesh.

Crossing the cultural barriers of race, religion, politics, social standing and geography for the sake of Christ is the example we emulate.

A serving church

The Word dwelt among us (v 14). The text 'Come out from among them and be separate' (2 Cor 6:17) has often been mis-used to justify disengagement from the world. Jesus touched lepers and ate with the marginalised, nor did he separate him-self from sinners, even on the cross. The church is at its most ef-fective when, without privilege, it serves the present age and fulfils its calling to servanthood by its Servant-King.

When a terrorist bomb killed and maimed people in the Shankill Road in Belfast, some asked 'Where was God?' The reply was in the question: 'Where was the church?' Some of the first people on the scene were the members of the Methodist church next door whose people and premises continued to serve the community with prayer and care and counsel by day and night. God was on the Shankill Road that dreadful day, in and through his people of all denominations.

The Christian mission is to transform sinful society and sin-ful individuals. As salt permeates food, and light penetrates darkness, so Christians are called to go into all the world to en-rich it and preserve its goodness and to dispel its darkness and point the way to its Saviour. John Stott notes how in 1835 G. B. Shaw and H. G. Wells with others founded the Fabian Society to make Britain socialist by a policy of infiltration. Wells later pro-nounced the policy a failure, saying it was 'as effective as a mouse may be said to permeate a cat'; it was swallowed up. Stott comments that it is not possible for Christians to perfect society, since we are not utopians (that must await the parousia only) but it is possible to improve society. Light and life are what the followers of Christ are meant to be until the earth is filled with the truth and glory of God.

Living the life, is a model for mission.

God cares enough to call us 'There was a man sent from God whose name was John.' (v 6)

How amazing it is that God calls fallible people with ordinary names like John or Jane to show his extraordinary nature of grace and forgiving love to all (v 14). The wonder is that we can hear and respond to God's call but the greater wonder is that in the first place God calls ordinary people like us. The challenge is that we should live our life as called, rather than driven people. God wants, not our ability, but our availability.

Sending people

The church is God's chosen instrument for the spreading of the gospel and the church is always only one generation away from extinction. God actually wants people for his work of spreading the kingdom in all the world. His commission is to go into all the world (Mt 28:19). There are various ways of going for we can go by praying, giving and by moving. The inescapable call is for the church, that is all believers, to go. I remember attending missionary rallies with the slogans 'have you God's permission to stay at home?' and debates on the subject 'is the need, the call?' Day by day we make ourselves available to Christ and follow him as we hear him saying 'Follow me.' The church is always in the business of commissioning mission partners.

Receiving people

The world is God's and he demonstrated his ownership of it when he came to Bethlehem in Jesus. People had no room for him. The church is God's and sometimes we have no room for those whom God has called and sent among us. John the Baptiser came from the desert and was unorthodox in his lifestyle, yet he came from God to make the way straight for the Lord. Those who were open to God received him but the religious establishment did not. God sends people from outside to pitch their tent in our churches and we are also called to receive them. Churches in the West are often less ready to receive missionaries from other cultures than they are to send them. Mission is about sending and receiving. It would be no bad thing if all churches, even in monochrome cultures, would aim to be multi-racial and international.

Caring people
Mission is costly and John the Baptiser was beheaded. We should treat well those whom God has called to minister to us. Some congregations eat their minister when they give the preacher a roasting at Sunday lunch. Grace and truth go together. Too often we have the truth but not the grace, which Stott says is 'love that cares and stoops and rescues.' May God give us both.

Going where we are sent is a model for mission.

Christians are called to share an active word, show a visible incarnation and spread a living presence in order to win the world for Christ.

Prayer:
O God,
enlarge my heart
that it may be big enough
to receive the greatness of your love.
Stretch my heart,
that it may take into it all those
who with me around the world
believe in Jesus Christ.
Stretch it,
that it may take into it
all those who do not know him,
but who are my responsibility
because I know him.
And stretch it,
that it may take in all those
who are not lovely in my eyes,
and whose hands I do not want to touch;
through Jesus Christ my Saviour. Amen.
from Africa

'Think again'*

Harold Miller

'I appeal to you, therefore, brothers and sisters,
by the mercy of God … present your bodies as a living sacrifice, holy
and acceptable to God, which is your spiritual worship.
Do not be conformed to the world,
but be transformed by the renewal of your minds.' Romans 12:1, 2

'Think again' has to be, first and foremost a message to the members of the church, as we re-think what it means to be part of God's people in our particular place at this particular time. We are to be a church which places at the top of our priorities the gospel message of reconciliation in a divided society. We are to be a church which, in an illustration I once heard, moves from being a circle of people holding hands looking inwards, to being a circle of people holding hands looking outwards, engaging with the needs of the community, and proclaiming the good news which welcomes the outsider with warmth and love. We are to be a church which passes on the message at the centre of our lives to generations still to come. And, as we dare to re-think our priorities before the Lord, so we are enabled to ask those around us who have been distanced from the church, bored by the church or put off by the church, to think again about how they view us, and more importantly how they see the Lord Jesus, the one at the heart of our very being.

I want to focus on the first two verses of Romans chapter 12. They begin with the words of Paul: 'I appeal to you, therefore, brothers and sisters, by the mercy of God …'

Family of God, those who are God's children, those who know and love the one Lord Jesus Christ, those who have re-

* Address at the launching of the diocesan strategy in Down & Dromore for the years 2000-2005.

ceived the wonderful grace and mercy of God, by which we have been forgiven and accepted by our heavenly Father ... Family of God, I appeal to you.

I am asking you to come with me on this journey, and to embrace the 'ROY' priorities of reconciliation, outreach and young people. Such priorities I believe are from God, and need to be our personal priorities. I plead with you, let the rubber hit the road in your parishes; I plead with you (because it has been suggested that we have chosen the three things we find most difficult to succeed in), not to give up when it becomes painful or difficult, but to look with me for the renewing power of the Holy Spirit by which alone we can live for God.

I appeal to you, by the mercies (or the compassion) of God, love your enemies, care for the poor and needy, go out into the world with the good news, and make it your priority to win young people for Christ, so that there may not grow up in our land a generation which does not know the Lord.

Now, how is this all to happen? The answer is, by thinking again ... fresh, new, vibrant, biblical and godly thinking. Paul puts it in these famous words: 'Do not be conformed to the world, but be transformed by the renewal of your minds.'

If I were to paint a picture of much of the 'unreconstructed' (to use a popular political word at the moment) church today, I might use the image of three different animals to illustrate the problem:

1. Sometimes the church has the characteristics of a chameleon

Chameleons have that incredible and fascinating ability to merge with the background. If they are on a leaf they will be green; on the sand, they will be sandy; on bark, brown; on concrete, grey. You are surprised when they move, because they have fitted their surroundings so well. Some churches and Christians are exactly like that – totally conformed to the world around, which it isn't difficult to be, so that nobody notices they are any different. I remember an unbelieving student at Queen's University, Belfast, pointing out to me that he was sick and tired of the church, because the people inside were no different to the people outside! If the society around is sectarian, the chameleon takes on orange or green; if it is hopeless and depressed, the chameleon becomes black; if it is wealthy and materialistic, the chameleon becomes gold.

2. Sometimes the church has the characteristics of an ostrich

What does an ostrich classically do? Sticks its head in the sand. Buries itself, so that it doesn't see what is happening around it, or only sees what it wants to see. Ostrich churches become like hermetically sealed bubbles, so much in the world of the other-worldly that they are of little earthly use. They do 'church' things in 'church' ways, and don't dare to engage with the dirti-ness and lostness of the world around. They become churches which trade in the grace which saves wretches, for the niceness which tidies up nice people. Comfortable and inward looking, unrelated to reality.

3. Sometimes the church has the characteristics of a lemming

I'm sure you've seen lemmings on TV programmes like *Survival*. The last lot I saw were throwing themselves over a cliff to sure and certain death. Little, vole-like creatures, who follow where everybody else is going even when it means their own destruc-tion. Do you know, it is possible for the church to become like that – even to prefer death to life. I could take you to at least one church where the major concern of many of the parishioners is to keep the graveyard open and untrodden upon, rather than to risk change which might bring life and a bit of untidiness with it!

Risking the possibility of carrying my zoological metaphors too far, might I suggest, from Romans 12, that God does not want the conformity of a chameleon church, the irrelevance of an os-trich church, the death-urge of a lemming church, but rather, the transformation of a *butterfly* church:

- Be transformed
- Be changed
- Allow yourselves to experience a metamorphosis!

How many members of the Anglican Church does it take to change a light-bulb? Answer: ten; one to change it and nine to say they preferred the old one. How many members of the Church of Ireland does it take to change a light-bulb? Answer: 'Change!? What's all this talk about change?!'

Change is at the very heart of the Christian message. Transforming change. When we talk about new birth, what can we mean but the most radical change in the world? When we talk about being converted, what can we mean but a totally new direction for our lives? When we talk about repentance, we probably don't know that the word means 'changing our minds.'

Paul says to the Christians at Rome: 'Go on being transformed by the renewal of your minds.' This change doesn't finish when we come into God's family. Instead, we go on and on and on being changed, from one degree of likeness to another, until we become more and more the people God wants us to be. That is the essence of the Christian life. A butterfly in its cocoon has potentially all the elements of a most beautiful and colourful creature, but it must allow itself to be completely transformed, if it is to emerge in all its glory and splendour.

Think again:

Allow your mind to be transformed by the Spirit and informed by God's word.

Think again:

So that, in the strength of the unchanging God, you can make a clear decision of the will to do what God wants for his church in this generation.

Think again:

So that you and I, and indeed the whole church, can repent of all the ways in which the world has squeezed us into its mould.

Think again:

So that your chosen priority can be (as we heard the Mothers Union in Southern Sudan sing) *Jesu No 1!*

Can you imagine the potential there is in the church of God?

Can you even dare to think of the difference we could make if we were out and out for God?

Can you dream of a transformed church, and will you be part of transforming it?

What, then, am I asking you to do? Here it is in the words of Paul: 'Present your bodies as a living sacrifice, holy and acceptable to God, which is your spiritual worship.' Nothing airy fairy: your bodies. I'll ask your bodies to stand to do that. Your bodies. Your mouths which speak out your faith, your relationships, your hands which do things and even spend your money, your eyes which express love, your minds which think, your feet which go places. Every single part of you.

We also stand as representatives of his body, the church, which looks to him as head, and commit ourselves to seek the will of Christ together, to dare to do it, so that people who come into our churches may see there something of the values of God's kingdom, and be drawn to serve him as their Lord.

Prayer:
I am no longer my own but yours.
Your will, not mine, be done in all things,
wherever you may place me,
in all that I do and in all that I may endure;
when there is work for me to do, and when there is none;
when I am troubled and when I am at peace;
Your will be done,
when I am valued and when I am disregarded;
when I find fulfilment, and when fulfilment is lacking;
when I have all things and when I have nothing.

I willingly offer all I have and am
to serve you, as and where you choose.

Glorious and blessed God,
Father, Son and Holy Spirit,
you are mine and I am yours.
So be it.
And this covenant now made on earth,
let it be fulfilled in heaven. Amen.

Jesus is the answer – but what's the question?

David Wilkinson

'He is before all things and in him all things hold together.' Colossians
1:17
Bible passage: Colossians 1:15-23

The late Rev Bill Gowland, Methodist evangelist and pioneer of
industrial mission, used to object strongly to people using the
phrase 'Jesus is the answer.' His point was simply that the
phrase did not make sense unless you defined the question. The
challenge of ministry in the new millennium is not as much
holding to Jesus as the all-embracing answer, as important as
that will be, but of understanding the questions.

The Christian church in the developed world is very good at
posing questions to the world. Yet sometimes we are slow in our
ministry to hear the questions which the world itself is asking. In
my own ministry in apologetics in the last few years, this passage from Colossians has taken on fresh significance as I have
heard the questions. Let me try and illustrate this.

First, the question 'How can we make the world a better
place?' This turn of the century is very different from the last
turn of the century in terms of optimism. In the year 1900, science and technology were triumphant. Evolution had explained
the diversity of the natural world and virtually all the questions
of physics seemed to be answered. The Eiffel Tower, cinema,
comics, the popular press, radio and the first modern Olympics
in Athens represented a time of romance, passion, art and technology. The provision of universal education and the power of
reason would make the world a better place, and there would be
no more war or suffering. Utopia of the twentieth century lay
ahead and it was only a matter of years before it was achieved.

However, the dream of human progress quickly turned into

nightmare. The diversity of life was eroded by abuse of the environment, human value was mocked in the gas chambers of Auschwitz and technology was used to kill millions in the horror of war. The power of reason, for all its achievements, did not lead inevitably to Utopia.

So how do we make the world a better place? Many at the beginning of the twenty-first century are asking that question, sometimes in the most unusual way. For example, the past decade has seen an explosion in interest in aliens, with the search for extraterrestrial intelligence, growth in science fiction and fascination with 'X-Files' phenomena such as alien visitation and abduction. There are many reasons for this explosion, but as far back as 1949, Sir Fred Hoyle pointed out the following motivation for believing in extraterrestrial intelligence, 'the expectation that we are going to be saved from ourselves by some miraculous interstellar intervention.'[1] One correspondent to the UFO magazine *Sightings* commented on what an encounter with aliens would mean, '… their positively vast medical technology could result in new medical techniques, ridding us of cancer or even AIDS. Possibly they could resolve our planet's famine and drought problems, and allow us to open our eyes and minds and discover the rest of the universe.' Within such all embracing optimism, it is surprising the correspondent did not also say, 'And find all the odd socks which go missing!'

Nevertheless, in answer to the question, 'How do we make the world a better place?' many look beyond themselves.

The second question is 'What is the purpose of it all?' As science has progressed more and more it has raised questions which lie beyond its own ability to answer. In particular, work on the origin of the universe has in recent years led many physicists to ask questions about the purpose of the Universe. When Stephen Hawking wrote *A Brief History of Time* no one expected how big a bestseller it would become. It has sold 5.5 million copies worldwide, given birth to a whole range of media spin-offs and given Professor Hawking the opportunity to star in *Star Trek, The Simpsons* and even spectacle commercials! The popularity of the book has much to do with Professor Hawking's own personal story, but it is much more than that. It probes questions at the interface of science and religion. Carl Sagan characterised the book as being about an absence of God, but that is far from the truth. After Hawking's magnificent exposition of quantum gravity, or the how the universe may have begun from a quantum fluctuation, he finishes by acknowledging that even a 'theory of everything' would not explain why the universe existed. He challenges philosophers to explore that question.

Paul Davies is another leading cosmologist fascinated with the question of purpose. Growing up in a Christian youth group he was unable to get answers to the deep questions about God and the universe he wanted to ask. He resolved that only science would give him true answers and so he devoted his life to science. Yet as he discovered more in science he found that science itself was raising questions of whether there is a deeper purpose to the universe. He writes:

> Through science we human beings are able to grasp at least some of the nature's secrets ... Why should this be? Just why *Homo Sapiens* should carry the spark of rationality that provides the key to the universe is a deep enigma. We who are children of the universe – animated stardust – can nevertheless reflect on the nature of the same universe, even to the extent of glimpsing the rules on which it runs – What is Man that we may be party to such privilege? I cannot believe that our existence in this universe is a mere quirk of fate, an accident of fate, an incidental blip in the great cosmic drama. Our involvement is just too intimate. The physical species *Homo* may count for nothing, but the existence of mind in some organism on some planet in the universe is surely a fact of fundamental significance ... This can be no trivial detail, no minor by-product of mindless purposeless forces. We are truly meant to be here.[2]

The third question is even more fundamental, 'What is God like?' Perhaps this is even more important than the question of whether God exists. Surveys suggest that up to 70% of people have some experience which they identify as experience of transcendence. Cosmologists as we have seen are led through questions of science to belief in a deeper purpose or designer of the universe. But what is the nature of the being behind the universe and spiritual experience? The increasing pluralism of contemporary society reinforces the question. In a world of so many different claims and diverse religions, what is God like?

Yet at every level, it is the type of question that should not be avoided. The phenomenal success of the *Star Wars* films of George Lucas can not be explained only in terms of the special effects. The stories themselves, with heroes, evil, hope and self-sacrifice, seem to strike a chord with people. In particular, Lucas raises the question of God in his concept of the 'Force'. He comments, 'I would hesitate to call the Force God … It's designed primarily to make young people think about mystery. Not to say, "here's the answer". It's to say "Think about this for a second. Is there a God? What does God look like? What does God sound like? What does God feel like? How do we relate to God?".'[3]

Thus one of the tasks of Christian ministry is to humbly listen to the questions. Then it is easier to see how the Christian message relates to the contemporary world.

Paul's letter to the Colossian Christians is such an exercise. We do not know a great deal about the Colossian church but it is possible that it began during Paul's prolific evangelistic ministry in Ephesus (Acts 19:8-10). Using the lecture hall of Tyrannus, Paul argued for the gospel every day for two years. So effective was his ministry that Luke claims, 'all the residents of Asia … heard the word of the Lord.' Possibly some from nearby Colossae heard the word of the Lord and went back and planted a church. Later a worker from that church named Epaphras visits Paul with good and bad news. The good news is that the church has 'love in the Spirit' (Col 1:8). The bad news is termed by New Testament scholars 'the Colossian heresy' and its nature has been the subject of much scholarly debate. While no one is certain of the details, the core of the heresy seems to have been the message 'Jesus is not that special!' False teachers were saying to the Christians that they needed secret knowledge or had to go through secret rituals in order to be really Christians. Paul saw in this a great danger because it misunderstood who Jesus was and what faith in him implied.

Paul's response to the type of questions that Epaphras brought him reaches its highpoint in his description of the supremacy of Christ. Paul's argument is simply that because Jesus is supreme in all things he is also sufficient for all things. Two thousand years later in a very different context, the message has relevance to us. In the questions that people ask, the supremacy of Jesus means that he is the sufficient answer. Let's pick out a few of the areas where Paul details the supremacy of Jesus where they relate to our own contemporary questions.

1. Jesus is supreme in revelation

A little girl was once painting a picture. Her mother came up and asked her what was she painting? The little girl replied, 'A picture of God.' 'But,' said her mother, 'No-one knows what God looks like!' 'They will,' replied the little girl, 'When they have seen the picture.'

In answer to the question 'What is God like?', Paul replies, 'He is like Jesus.' Jesus is the 'image of the invisible God' (v 15), the projection of God himself into the dimensions of space-time in a way that reveals his true nature. If we want to see what God is like, we look at the image.

Yet, images by themselves can be quite misleading. Someone on seeing a photograph of our daughter Hannah commented on what a placid child she seemed to be. However, at the age of three she is far from placid! Paul does not say that Jesus is simply a representation of God. Later in the passage he claims that in Jesus 'all the fullness of God was pleased to dwell' (v 19). Jesus is more than just an image, he is God himself walking among us.

Although God reveals himself in many and various ways, he reveals himself supremely in the man born 2000 years ago in a stable in Bethlehem. For those searching for the nature of God, or questioning the nature of God following some kind of bad experience, Christian ministry encourages the person to engage with Jesus through the reading of the gospels and by trusting in him as Lord and Saviour.

2. Jesus is supreme in creation

Paul's cosmic description of Jesus echoes the understanding of 'wisdom' in some of the Old Testament. There God creates the world through wisdom. Here the creative work of God is expressed not through a concept but through a person. Jesus is before creation, he is the foundation of creation, he is the agent of creation and he is the answer to the question of the purpose of creation (vv 15-16). In addition, he is the sustainer of creation for 'in him all things hold together' (v 17). Just as the head and hands of a sculptor are together in creating something beautiful, so God the Father and God the Son are together in the work of creation.

This would have had an immediate application to the Colossian Christians. The ancient world was often obsessed with intermediaries between heaven and earth – principalities, authorities, demons and angels. Paul is saying that even if these things existed then they were all created by Jesus and, therefore, if you have faith in him, there is no need to be either obsessed or fearful about these things.

In our own time, this understanding of Jesus has a great deal to say to those looking for purpose in the universe. Science explores a universe which has a faithfulness to it represented in the laws of physics. However, science can never explain where these laws come from, it simply assumes that they are there. Paul says that the universe 'holds together' or 'coheres' not because of an impersonal physical theory but because of the creative work of Jesus. Science is only possible because of the work of Jesus.

Therefore, Christian ministry can affirm science and technology. Those who explore the universe or exploit its order in technology or engineering, do so because the universe 'holds together'.

Such work is Christian ministry as much as evangelism or preaching. In addition, Christian ministry encourages those who are looking for a deeper purpose to the universe than science itself can give to engage with the person of Jesus.

3. Jesus is supreme in reconciliation

Paul now moves on to speak of Jesus as supreme in reconciliation (v 20). We are well used to the term 'reconciliation'. It presupposes some kind of separation or division which needs to be overcome. Imagine two people having a conversation as they approach a division in the road. If one decides to go to the right and the other decides to go to the left, immediately a separation forms and their communication comes to an end.

In the same way, the biblical message is that men and women were created by God to be in intimate relationship with him. However, we have decided to go our own way without him thus forming a separation between God and ourselves. The Bible goes further to say that this alienation from God is the source of what is wrong with the world. Alienation from God leads to alienation from one another and our abdication of responsibility to care for the world.

Yet the death of Jesus bridges that separation, making peace through his self-sacrifice. While the actual mechanics of what is going on here may be beyond us, we know from our own experience that reconciliation costs. In our case that cost may be pride or some things we hold dear which must be sacrificed for reconciliation to happen. Jesus willingly gives his own life on the cross in order to take the cost of our rebellion and restore us to a right relationship with God.

The extent of this reconciliation is total. Paul uses a parallel in verses 19 and 20. As nothing of the fullness of God was left out of Jesus, so nothing is beyond his reconciling work. No one person or no one situation is beyond the cross.

Christian ministry needs to hold fast to that as it addresses the question of how the world may be made a better place. The reasons for particular situations in the world today are complex, but none are beyond the reconciling work of Christ. Indeed, only through reconciliation with God can lasting peace be achieved. The extent of this reconciliation is total but not automatic. Women and men, organisations and governments need to turn to God through repentance and faith.

It is God alone who can give hope for the new millennium. Far from putting our hope in alien visitors in the far future, the cross of Jesus stands as a historical testimony to the reality of reconciliation.

Conclusion

Paul's answer to the Colossian heresy is the supremacy of Jesus in revelation, in creation and in reconciliation. The same understanding of Jesus gives the answer to some of today's questions. Yet the supremacy of Jesus goes beyond just being an answer. It poses a further question.

Charles Simeon was an Anglican minister in Cambridge. One of his final sermons was preached on this passage from Colossians. As he came to Colossians 1:18, it is said that Simeon's old frame visibly straightened in the pulpit and he said, 'That in all things he might have the pre-eminence. And he must have it; and he will have it; and he shall have it.' Many in the congregation suddenly saw in this old man of God a challenge which was that if Jesus was supreme in all things, was he supreme in all things in their individual lives.

In Christian ministry I may proclaim Jesus as supreme in revelation, creation and reconciliation, but is he supreme in my ambition, my relationships, my use of money and my assessment of myself? That is a question which I need to live with day by day.

Prayer:

Lord of all things, be Lord in my life today. May you have the supremacy in all of the decisions in my life. Give me your grace to help me to listen to you and to others. Help me to see you at work in the world and to be sensitive to the questions of those around me. Thank you, Lord Jesus, for all the things you have done for us, most of all for your death on the cross. May others acknowledge your supremacy and may my ministry be used in answering this prayer. Amen.

1. F. Hoyle, *Monthly Notices of the Royal Astronomical Society*, 109, 365, 1949.
2. Davies, *The Mind of God*, Simon & Schuster, 1992, p. 173.
3. B. Moyers & G. Lucas, 'Of Myth and Men', *Time*, 26 April 1999.

Courage for the new millennium

Duleep Fernando

*'Now, Lord, consider their threats and enable your servants
to speak your word with great boldness.' Acts 4:29*

1. At the crossroads

The early Christians had a crisis. Peter and John had healed the
crippled man at the gate of the temple in Jerusalem. The next
day they were arrested by the authorities and hauled before the
Sanhedrin, Israel's highest court. They were told that they must
not speak or teach at all in the name of Jesus. They were threatened and released. They went back to the infant church and re-
ported to them the threats that were made. There were fears of
persecution and even extinction.

The options are clear. They can remain quiet and be an inward looking church, meeting regularly for worship and study
among themselves, or they can move out and preach boldly the
good news of Jesus. The choice was between security and maturity, stagnation and growth, between looking after themselves or
reaching out to others. We see their response in the prayer in
verse 25: 'Now; Lord, consider their threats and enable your servants to speak your word with great boldness.' The choice is
made. They will not hide in fear and protect themselves. They
will reach out and preach the word to others.

This same choice comes to us as a church in the third millennium: to remain in our comfort zones – to protect ourselves; to
remain in our little grooves, doing those things that we have always done, or to take risks, to launch out into the deep, to have
the courage to change, to see new visions and go on uncharted
paths.

When an eagle has its young, it keeps them in its nest high up
in a tree or rock. After a few weeks, the mother eagle decides to

teach the eaglets to fly. She pushes them one by one out of her nest. At first, the baby eagle clutches desperately to the nest but is ruthlessly pushed out and as it falls, it starts using its wings and learns to soar up into the skies. This is true of the church. We can remain in our comfortable nests, secure and safe from the troubles, conflicts and challenges of the world. But, God pushes us out from our established ways and, when we trust him and launch out, we have power to rise with wings of an eagle. 'They who wait upon the Lord shall renew their strength, they shall mount up with wings as eagles' (Is 40:31). It is my hope that the church will soar to see new visions, attempt new possibilities, rise to new challenges and stretch out in new directions.

Christians need to see new visions. In every life, there is a moment when we see a vision of a higher and a worthier life with greater service to God and of greater usefulness to God's kingdom. To realise that vision, we need courage to break away from our accustomed lifestyle and leave the nest and take risks. For some, the cost is too great and they never realise that vision. They go on in the established path of safety and never leave their comfort zone. It can happen to any Christian and any church. We find our spiritual life is empty. We have no real experience of God and no lives are changed in our church. The power of God is not evident. Young people are not challenged to take the claims of Christ seriously. There is no assurance or confidence that God is there in our midst, and we just keep going the way we have always gone. God can change our vision and our lives and revive the church. The Holy Spirit brought order out of chaos in creation. In this age, he often reverses his role. He disturbs our settled and established lives and causes chaos in our order. Are we prepared for upheaval?

I was recently in a village in the south of Sri Lanka. A young evangelist, living in a spiritually dry and difficult area, had a deep hunger to see the power of God at work in a way that was different from the usual Sunday services with a few loyal members quietly worshipping God. He fasted and prayed for forty days and organised a four-day revival programme with open air meetings. I spoke on the last day to a full crowd. I was recovering from illness and felt weak and was asking myself whether I should be there, but when I went there, I saw the power of the Spirit at that meeting and I felt as if I was carried by God's Spirit. I felt as if I was in a boat and all I had to do was to put up the sails to be driven by the wind of the Spirit. God can do this everywhere.

2. On our knees

When the early church was faced with this threat they prayed. If we had to face that kind of threat in our churches, we would have first summoned a church council or informed the police or spoken to a politician or, perhaps, taken an insurance policy on our building against riots and civil commotion. These believers came together and prayed. This was God's work and had to be done in his power and according to his will. It was a prayer to the Living God who would act in this situation.

I personally believe that prayerlessness is one of the worst sins of the church because it shows who we really think is in charge of the world and of the church. If we think this is God's business and he is in control, we will pray. 'If we are too busy to pray, then we are too busy.'

This was the source of their courage. They prayed to a God who answered prayer; who said 'Call on me and I will answer you and tell you great and unsearchable things you do not know' (Jer 33:3). Someone said, 'Courage is fear that has said its prayers.' In times of danger and risk, there is bound to be fear, but when we pray we know that God is there for us and he will work out his purposes, and this banishes our fear.

3. Ready for action

As we look at the content of their prayer, we would have thought that in the face of threats and persecution, they would have prayed for safety and protection. Not so. They prayed, 'Oh Lord, consider their threats and enable your servants to speak the word with great boldness.' Courage is what they asked for.

That is what the church in Sri Lanka needs more than anything else in the new millennium. Sometimes we hear of workers giving up on their call because they are de-motivated or discouraged, or we have members facing tragedy, failure and suffering and deciding to give up on God. Now we need courage to keep going without giving up. 'When the going gets tough, the tough get going.' As we look at their prayer, we see the source of their courage.

3.1 Sovereignty of God

The prayer starts, 'Sovereign Lord, you have made the heaven and the earth and the sea and everything in them.' They believed in a God who was sovereign, who was Lord of creation, redemption, history and the present. The great 'I am', to whom ultimate power and control belongs. God is unchanged and unchanging. Whatever happens, God is in control. His purposes will triumph. Dictators and tyrants will strut around the stage of life as if absolute power belongs to them. But the Hitlers, Stalins, Pol Pots, Idi Amins, will see their finitude, their limitations and mortality and in a moment they will be gone and they will be remembered no more. Only God is Lord. Only his kingdom is eternal. Nothing can defeat his purposes because absolute power belongs to him.

3.2 God has spoken

These believers found courage because they knew a God who had spoken. 'You spoke by the Holy Spirit through the mouth of your servant, our father David' (v 25).

This God has revealed himself to us. He has made his will known. He has spoken to his people through his prophets, his apostles and his Son. So often we are uncertain of ourselves and lack courage because we do not know God's will. We do not know what our stand should be on an issue because, unlike the prophets of old, we are unable to say 'Thus says the Lord.' As a church we have to ask ourselves the question, 'Have we faith in the Bible, as the word of God?' In the midst of all the relativism and the conflicting voices on moral issues, we will lose our way as Christians if we can not turn to the Bible as our ultimate authority on matters of faith and practice. Often Christians are woefully ignorant of basic Christian truths and principles.

We need people who will reveal God's word to us and restore our confidence in the Bible as a credible guide to truth. We need to show that the principles spelt out in the Bible are authentic and practical for our day and age and show us the path to victorious living. If the church does not have the word of God as its compass, we will lose our way in the new millennium and become an irrelevant voice among the Babel of voices. The call goes out to our churches to teach our people and equip them so that they can face life with all its complexities with the truths of God's word in their minds and hearts.

3.3 The sinfulness of people

These first believers believed in the Sovereignty of God, but they also knew that because of the freedom given to man, he can do evil and even try to subvert the plans of God. 'Evil men conspired against God's Holy Son and nailed him to a cross,' but God even used their sin to fulfil what he had decided to do for the redemption of the world. These first believers were realistic about the human condition. They had no illusions about human sin and the suffering it would bring. We too need to be realistic about the advanced technology and the explosion of knowledge and the spread of miracle drugs, but the fallen nature of man will use these blessings that science and technology bring, not just for human welfare, but also for human oppression and exploitation. Internet and Satellite Communication bring vast stores of knowledge to our doorsteps but they will also bring perverse pictures and decadent ideologies to our homes. We fool ourselves if we think sinful human beings will eliminate pain, suffering and sorrow in the new millennium. If the old is anything to go by, the benefits of these technologies will be enjoyed by a few and the rich will get richer while the poor get poorer. In every age humankind needs a Saviour to save us from ourselves and our own boasting self-confidence and short-sighted wisdom. We need to be saved from our fallen nature. Jesus Christ is that Saviour who can transform individuals and social life and bring salvation and liberation. Our calling is to speak the word of God with boldness to our contemporary situation. We analyse contemporary society and relate the gospel to it and point to the Saviour who alone can give full salvation.

3.4 Signs and wonders

Their last request in their prayers was that God would stretch out his hand to heal and perform miraculous signs and wonders. They wanted to show the world that God was alive and at work. Even though the sin of man does its worst, God will work out his purposes so that all things work together for good to those who love God (Rom 8:28). In Sri Lanka today we are seeing more manifestations of signs and wonders in the ministry of the church, including miracles of healing and exorcism. There is no doubt that these manifestations of the power of God break down the defences and prejudices that people have to the gospel. People are hungry for evidences of the divine. God can use signs and wonders to open the eyes of people blinded by materialism and prejudice. We pray for this form of ministry. We must use all the means available to proclaim with boldness, the Living God revealed in Jesus Christ.

Conclusion

The church is always called to courage, change and faith. We need courage to change, and wisdom to hold on to those eternal realities that are unchanging. The impact of globalisation is a challenge to our cultures, economy and way of life. The church will be challenged to use new methods to present the gospel and interpret it to the people of our age. John Wesley rode on horseback and preached to the crowds in the open air. We will use modern methods of communication. Yet there are things that will not change. The nature of man will not change. Made in the image of God, he will rise to great heights of creativity and innovation. Yet as a fallen creature and as a sinner, he needs the grace of God and he needs a Saviour to save him from the ill effects of his sin. Let us fearlessly proclaim Jesus Christ the Saviour. The Word of God will not change. Its interpretation and application will change, but as Christ said 'Heaven and earth will pass away my word will not pass away.' It must remain our guide and authority. The gospel of Jesus Christ will not change. Humankind will remain a cosmic orphan who is lost in God's universe unless we find our place and meaning in this world through a personal relationship with God in Jesus Christ. Lastly, Jesus Christ will not change. He is the same yesterday, today and forever. He is the Lord of history from whom we date our era. Christ is at the centre stage of history. One day he will bring this age to a close. As the Creed says: 'He will come again to judge both the living and the dead' when he will inaugurate a new age with 'a kingdom that shall have no end'. We must be ready to meet him whenever he comes and our great business as a church till he comes, is to tell the millions who have never known his love, that God is alive and he cares for them. One day, every knee shall bow and every tongue will confess that Jesus Christ is Lord to the glory of the Father, but till then, let us declare with boldness, the good news of his salvation.

The church needs more than any thing else, courageous people who will put Christ first in their lives and be the salt of the earth and the light of the world.

Prayer:
God of grace and God of glory
On thy people pour thy power;
Crown thine ancient church's story;
Bring her bud to glorious flower.
Grant us wisdom, grant us courage
For the facing of this hour.
H. E. Fosdick

The ministry of reconciliation

David W. Porter

'*Truth and mercy will meet; justice and peace will kiss each other*'
(Psalm 85:10)

ECONI (Evangelical Contribution on Northern Ireland) emerged
in response to a growing crisis in the Protestant community in
Northern Ireland. The Anglo-Irish Agreement of 1985 was seen
by the overwhelming majority of Protestants as a real political
threat to their national identity. For many the agreement implied an equally serious challenge to their religious identity,
which had become synonymous with the unionist cause.

The bombing of a remembrance service in Enniskillen in 1988
struck at the heart of a Protestant community that considered itself under attack by terrorists, betrayed by government and misunderstood in the wider world. The expression of forgiveness
by Gordon Wilson, a Methodist lay preacher and the father of
one of the victims, not only offered a beacon of hope, but ignited
a debate among many Evangelicals about the nature of forgiveness and reconciliation.

This debate has continued to impact the response of Evangelicals to the developing peace process. The Belfast Agreement
of 1998 provoked vigorous debate within the Protestant churches,
with many viewing the provision for the release of prisoners as a
bridge too far in the search for peace and reconciliation. Others
have been equally convinced of the value of the agreement as an
instrument of reconciliation in a deeply divided community.
This remains the reality among Evangelicals, with passions running high as the process unmasks the hard issues that must be
faced if the future is to offer any hope of a lasting settlement.

In this context, ECONI has been serving the church, equip-
ping Christians to respond biblically to living in a divided soci-

ety. This has involved us in a range of initiatives in both the church and community – resourcing believers to engage with the search for peace and engaging ourselves with community and political leaders in order to make a contribution to the peace process.

Religion has become the convenient label to use in describing the two sides of our conflict. As Christians we have to accept that while it has not been a religious war, religion has contributed to the fear, hate and mistrust that has marked our conflict of nationality and culture. Therefore our task in witnessing to the prince of peace is difficult. Reconciliation remains an elusive goal. The trauma of the last thirty years compounds the historic sense of grievance that both sides feel. War weariness and not the embrace of reconciliation is the primary driver of the peace. A tolerant coexistence may be the best we can expect from a community where wounds run deep and hatred is kept alive by the insistence that we are different from them.

Many historians are already designating the twentieth century as the most violent in human history. Never have the lives of so many people been affected by war. For the first time, more civilians have died in the wars of the twentieth century than have soldiers. And all this has occurred on a global scale, leaving no continent untouched by the horror of modern warfare.

In Europe, the human capacity for evil and violence has been demonstrated in the most horrific manner. Yet even here the great industrial wars of the century are but a cover for the intense conflict of national identity that is at the heart of tensions around the globe. The conflict in Ireland embraces the twentieth century in Europe like a pair of bookends. The century began with increasing tension in Ireland. Were it not for the start of hostilities in Europe, this threatened to bring civil war to the heart of the British Empire. The century has drawn to a close with thirty years of terrorism in Ireland dominating the news headlines with the unfinished business of an empire long past.

Events in Eastern Europe in the last decade have shown that Ireland, far from being the exception, has probably been an accurate reflection of the tension in relationships throughout the continent. This tension exists between the call to solidarity with our people and the call to embrace the diversity of others. It is the choice between obedience to the ancestral voices of our traditions and obedience to the market and free trade.

At a deeply spiritual level, it is the tension between remembering the hurt of our people at the hands of others and healing the wounds that threaten to overwhelm us in a cycle of vengeance. For the Christian, this spiritual challenge is at the heart of our call to discipleship. To follow Jesus is to declare ourselves under a new loyalty to the kingdom of God and committed to a new currency of reconciliation that enables us to embrace diversity and celebrate our common humanity in the grace of God. This is the call to be the people of God.

This is the challenge of reconciliation, where we remember and forgive, bringing about the redemption of God. In a world where identity conflicts will grow in both number and intensity, it is our ability as Christians to address these concerns that will determine the credibility of our witness into the twenty first century.

In order to understand how we can be a people of reconciliation, we need to reflect on what we have learnt about reconciliation in Ireland. The lessons come not from our success but our failure. Three pictures come to mind.

Called to be a place of reconciliation

In Psalm 85:10 we read: 'Truth and mercy will meet; justice and peace will kiss each other.' This psalm has been read in conflict negotiations in South Africa, the Middle East, Central America and Ireland. It is the peacemakers' psalm. In this verse we get a picture of God's salvation, of what it means for God to speak peace to his people. We have a crossroads where four characters meet – truth, mercy, justice and peace. This place is called reconciliation. Each of them has to be present, bringing their unique contribution to the process of reconciliation.

But this is not an abstract picture for it is the reality of God's redemption in history. Such reconciliation is a place in the past, that point where God's truth and mercy, justice and peace meet and embrace in the crucified Christ. But it is also a place in the future, the new heavens and earth created at that point in time and space when Jesus returns. It is Jesus who will fulfil the desires, aspirations and longings of all the peoples, cultures and tribes of our world. A new city with a tree of life, the leaves of which are for the healing of the nations.

Yet reconciliation is also a place in the present and that place is the church. God's people, a new human community where Jesus is Lord, forgiveness is the cure for vengeance, reconciliation the alternative to fear and hostility. This is the hardest challenge. For reconciliation is not simply what we aspire to as Christians, it is what we are as community.

Called to be on a pilgrimage of reconciliation

At the beginning of that crucial week in the gospel story, Luke tells us of Jesus, weeping over Jerusalem, crying out: 'If you, even you had only recognised on this day the things that make for peace! But now they are hidden from your eyes' (Lk 19:42). The implication is that it is possible to know what makes for peace. It may be hidden but it can be discovered. And that discovery involves us being willing to embark on a journey, for the second picture of reconciliation is that it is a pilgrimage.

It is a pilgrimage from hurt to healing that begins with Jesus in the place of lament. 'Reconciliation in the evangelical sense,' says Annemie Bosch, 'is not built on forgetting but on remembering.' To begin the journey we must acknowledge our wounds and grieve for the hurt of our people, as did Jesus and Jeremiah before him.

But Jesus our healer has a more disturbing lesson for us. Here as the victim, Jesus weeps over the wounds of the victimiser. The city that is about to crucify him will see judgement for their inability to recognise the time of their visitation from God. For Jesus this is a cause not of delight but of lament.

The hardest part of reconciliation is our ability not only to grieve for our own wounds, but also to acknowledge the wounds of our enemy and weep for their hurt. Furthermore, a test of true Christian reconciliation is that the initiative for reconciliation begins with the victim. It is God who is in Christ reconciling a world that has rebelled and rejects the divine rule. Jesus, the truly innocent victim, becomes the vehicle for the reconciliation of the truly guilty party.

'In Christian reconciliation,' says Bosch, 'we always have two parties – the perpetrator who remembers his guilt and therefore repents, and the victim who remembers his suffering but in spite of this forgives.' The reality in the sinful complexity of our tribal conflicts is that we can be both perpetuator and victim, called to repent and forgive based on a profound remembering of the hurts of both.

Called to be part of a process of reconciliation
The division in Ireland is not in the constitution or a line drawn on a map, but in the hearts and minds of the people. Paul's declaration in Romans 12:2, 'be transformed by the renewing of your minds', gives us our final picture. God is in the business of transforming hearts and renewing minds. Reconciliation is a process, an ongoing transformation at the heart of our being and communities that results in God's will being done on earth as in heaven.

At the centre of this process is repentance. When Jesus came his essential message was 'Repent, for the Kingdom of God is near.' Repentance in a community must begin with God's people. It must start with an acknowledgement that for too long we have created God in our own culture-bound image and have been paralysed in our effectiveness in response to the idols of our tribes which have nurtured the conflicts of our world, tending but not healing our wounds.

Furthermore, Jesus calls us into new relationships with all those around us, relationships built on love, *agape*, a committed act of the will to give ourselves for the good of others. And Jesus specifically calls us to love our enemies. It is on this basis that we can begin to build trust and work for justice (Lk 6). It is in this that we fulfil the law of God (Lk 10) and it is the offence of this that is the stumbling block to faith (Lk 4).

Jesus was not an escapist. He faced the realities of his context. He accepted the legitimate expression of cultural, political and national preferences. Jesus did not deny these, but redefined them (Lk 9). This involved Jesus in taking risks. Jesus risked the embrace of the prostitute, the touch of the leper, the friendship of the tax collector, the service of the centurion. He challenged the vested interests of privilege and power that militate against walking in the way of peace.

The calling of the church

This vision is a vision for the church. The people of God are called to be a place, to be on a pilgrimage and to be part of a process, the common theme of which is reconciliation. This is our responsibility in a broken world. We must avoid the danger of expecting society and the wider community to live as though it was the redeemed church. We must be passionate in our commitment to ensure the church is not allowed to live as though it was the unredeemed community. As those who in Christ have been reconciled to God, we share a new reality, the revolutionary potential of the kingdom of God in which all things are being made new.

> *Prayer:*
> God, you have set us apart
> as citizens of your kingdom
> in which righteousness and justice reign.
> Yet we confess that at times we only see
> the injustices against ourselves
> and are only concerned with our rights.
> But you require of us the courage
> To embrace the hurt and loss of others
> and the grace to listen to their story.
> Help us to create a space for them,
> to act justly and to love mercy,
> and to walk humbly with you. Amen.

The healing ministry in the church

John Horner

'...he sent them out to proclaim the kingdom of God and to heal.'
Luke 9:2

In Luke 9:2 (and elsewhere) we read that the commission of the disciples was two-fold, – to preach and heal. From Acts 3:6 (and elsewhere) it is clear that the apostles saw this commission to the two-fold ministry as still applying after the ascension. I submit that our separation of these two commands and our widespread neglect of the second, has had the following sad results:

God has been deprived of glory due to his name;
Jesus has been deprived of one of the benefits of his passion;
the Holy Spirit has been deprived of a sphere of operation;
the church has been deprived of credibility;
the world has been deprived of a remedy for its suffering;
the individual Christian has been deprived of joy and satisfaction.

Of course, God receives glory from other aspects of his people's worship, but how often do we hear the surge of thankful praise rising up from those who have been healed?

Of course, there are other benefits constantly received from the passion of Jesus, but he was not only 'wounded for our transgressions and crushed for our iniquities', he has also 'borne our infirmities and carried our disease', and 'by his bruises we are healed' – from our sickness as well as our sin (Is 53:4-5).

Of course, the Holy Spirit has other spheres of operation, notably in the work of regeneration, but this is no reason to deprive him of showing his power to the glory of God in works of healing.

Of course, there are many reasons why the church has lost credibility, But when we go on telling people that God can do all things but rarely show God doing anything, it is no wonder they don't take us seriously.

Of course, the world has many agencies within it working for the relief of its suffering, but the vast healing resources given by God through the authority of Jesus in the power of the Holy Spirit are largely unreleased.

And of course, Christians can and do receive satisfaction and joy through many forms of Christian service, but there is nothing quite as rewarding as having been used by God to bring healing, peace and liberty to someone in pain, turmoil and bondage.

But we should look for the arguments supporting the practice of the healing ministry, not so much in terms of the benefits of its results, as in the teaching and practice of Jesus, interpreted and expressed in the theology of the New Testament church. Paul wrote, 'Now you are the body of Christ' (1 Cor 12:27). Christians of all denominations would agree that the church is the body of Christ. And they would agree that the 'you' of Paul's statement refers to the local fellowship of believers (in this instance, the believers in Corinth) as well as to the church universal. But while most Christians accept this as a doctrine, how many work out and apply its tremendous implications? As the church is the body of Christ, it has the qualities and properties of that body, one of which is to be used by God in the ministry of healing. Sent by God, the Holy Spirit indwelt and reached out through the flesh of Christ to bring about the healing of God's people. We of the church are Christ's flesh today. The same Spirit indwells us and we, in his power, are given authority in the name of Jesus, to exercise the same ministry.

It is clear from Acts 3 that the apostles believed that the commission to heal still applied and that the power to do so was still available. Confronted by the lame man at the gate of the temple, Peter had no hesitation in claiming healing in the name of Jesus: 'What I have I give you, in the name of Jesus Christ of Nazareth, stand up and walk.' And the man jumped up and walked (Acts 3:7-8).

As we read on through Acts we see that the healing ministry was both the proof and the promotion of the gospel. That it was the proof is shown in the events that followed the healing just referred to. After the miracle, Peter was examined by the authorities on what he was up to. He gave it them straight from the shoulder, but it wasn't what Peter said that silenced the opposition, but 'When they saw the man who had been healed standing beside them, they had nothing to say in opposition' (Acts 4:14).

And, as I suggested, the miracles of healing were not only the proof of the gospel, they were also its promotion. 'Awe came upon everyone because many signs and wonders were being done by the apostles ... and day by day the Lord added to their number those who were being saved' (Acts 2:43, 47). 'Now many signs and wonders were done among the people through the apostles ... [and] more than ever believers were added to the Lord' (Acts 5:12, 14). There was no need for an advertising drive or a publicity campaign to promote church growth. The preaching of the gospel authenticated by the miracles that accompanied it, was all that was needed.

So already, by the time we reach the fourth chapter of Acts, we see God getting the glory due to his name, Jesus realising the benefits of his passion, the Holy Spirit released into full liberty, the church gaining credibility, the world receiving relief from its suffering and individual Christians rejoicing in their service and witness.

So why has the church so neglected the commission to heal? There are many reasons why this is so and there is no space to list them here. One is that the practice has been so much abused. But so has preaching and so has evangelism and so has social service. Surely the right reaction to abuse is not non-use, but correct use.

Now, it is important to remember that when we talk about healing we mean wholeness. Wholeness is God's will for us – the word comes from the same root as that for holiness. And wholeness includes healing not only of the body, but also of the mind, of memories, of relationships, and of the emotions – fear, anxiety, guilt and so on. Healing of the kind we are concerned with here is not offered to replace at all times and in all circumstances the healing available through medicine, surgery, psychiatry and the rest, but to complement it. And it must be acknowledged that there are some diseases and afflictions for which there is no known cure outside the ministry of the Holy Spirit.

To return to the plea for the correct use, as distinct from the non-use, of this ministry, it is vital that a church which offers a healing ministry should observe certain disciplines and be on its guard against making those blunders which can lead to disillusionment and distress. Above all, sufferers who do not receive what they ask for must not be dismissed with the impression that the fault is theirs: that they have been rejected by God because of their lack of faith, or their unworthiness, or because their sickness is a punishment for sin. To build up the faith and expectancy of sufferers by assuring them that God can do all things, without warning them that this is not the same as saying that God will do anything, can be disastrous. My experience over many years of involvement in this ministry, is that to the hundreds of people to whom I have ministered, there was not always given instant, complete and permanent cure. Many did receive just that, and we praise God for it, but those who did not receive it had been so prepared for the ministry, that they did not go away with a desolate disappointment, or a crushing burden of guilt. All testified to having received some help, some strength, some blessing that they did not have before.

Turning to some practical issues, I should like to offer the following observations:

1. The healing ministry, however structured or exercised, should be part of the ministry of every church. Assuming that God wants to use each local church in this way, he will have endowed its members with the resources and gifts necessary for the task. Paul makes this point in his first letter to the Corinthians when he says that each member of the body has been given a gift for the common good and in the list that follows he includes healing and miracles (1 Cor 12:4-11).

If every church included the healing ministry on its regular agenda, there would be less support and need for the 'Special Healing Mission' – a practice which was shunned by Jesus and for which there is no biblical warrant, but which has filled the vacuum created by the neglect of the churches.

2. The healing ministry should not only be on the agenda of every church, but it should be a regular and frequent feature of it. To have to tell sufferers that you may be able to help them, but not until your next healing service is due and you don't know when that will be, is, to say the least, not very satisfactory.

3. As the healing ministry is offered by and through the body of Christ, it is appropriate that a representative group of people should be actually involved in the laying-on of hands and the anointing with oil, rather than one person acting on his or her own. 'Solo' performances can give a false impression – e.g. that the 'performer' is on an 'ego trip', and can also lay on such a person an undue sense of personal pride – or, if what is asked for is not given – of guilt. Having said that, it should also be noted that there are exceptions. There are times when it is right for the ministry to be given in a one-to-one relationship. It would seem that certain people have a ministry (as distinct from a gift) of healing and these have a special anointing to act on their own. And there may also arise emergency situations within which a Christian must claim and exercise the gift of healing there and then. But 'solo performances' are the exception to the general rule. James, instructing the church on how to proceed when a request for healing is received, also makes the point that the agent of healing should not go it alone. He says that the 'elders' (note the plural) should be sent for. In some churches this may mean those trained and trusted with the healing ministry (Jas 5:14).

4. As to the form which the ministry will take, this may vary according to those exercising it. The laying-on of hands and anointing with oil are referred to in scripture. And, of course, prayer. I have found that a brief and stereotyped prayer repeated 'along the line' without specific reference to the need or request of the sufferer, is not as effective as an extended prayer time in

which the whole healing group takes part and which can include repentance, the receiving of forgiveness, praise, thanksgiving, declaration of faith and expectancy, and specific petition directed at the affected area in which healing is requested.

To sum up, then: the church is commissioned to continue the healing work of Jesus. As the body of Christ it has the authority and power to do this work. The healing ministry is both the proof and the promotion of the gospel. Over the years, the healing ministry has been abused, but our response to this should be correct use, not non-use. Persons asking for healing should be properly taught or counselled before the ministry takes place. The healing ministry should be a regular and frequent feature of the ministry of every church. The actual act of ministry should normally be performed by a group of people representing the church to which they belong. The Bible indicates that the ministry should include the laying-on of hands, the anointing with oil and prayer.

Prayer:
Loving God,
in whom all things are made whole,
you sent you Son our Saviour
to heal a broken world.
Visit us with your salvation,
that we may be blessed
in body, mind and spirit;
through Jesus Christ our Lord. Amen.
Methodist Worship

The beginning of worship

Desmond Bain

Suggested readings: Genesis 4:1-16, Romans 11:33-12:2

In the film, *The Sound of Music,* the Von Trapp children are being taught to sing by their governess, Sister Maria. The song she teaches to help them learn the basics has the words:

When you read you begin with A, B, C,

When you sing you begin with doh, ray, me ...

We might add, for our purposes, 'When you worship you begin with Sac-ri-fice'!

The story in Genesis of Cain and Abel bringing their sacrifices to God, is about how God is to be worshipped. It is a story, which like many in the book, bristles with problems, such as 'What kind of God prefers a little lamb being slaughtered to a sheaf of nourishing grain?' or 'Why did he like Abel more than Cain?' Whatever the difficulties we may see, we might begin to solve some of them when we realise that the Bible is telling us about ourselves – about what we offer to God, and how we offer it.

But before we look at the sacrifices we might make, let us glean some truths from Genesis chapter four. God sees what we do not. He saw first the person bringing the gift. Verse 4 says that, 'the Lord looked on Abel and his offering'. When the prophet Samuel went to anoint a king in succession to Saul, there were seven sons of Jesse brought out to him. When he saw Eliab, the eldest, he thought that because of Eliab's height and bearing, he must be the one whom God had chosen. The same was true of all the others. But the word of the Lord came to Samuel, 'Do not consider his appearance or his height, for I have rejected him. The Lord does not look at the things man looks at. Man looks at the outward appearance, but the Lord looks on the heart.'

The prophet Amos underlines that no gift is acceptable to God, if we do not also bring our sincere search for justice for others. 'I hate, I despise your religious feasts; I cannot stand your assemblies. Even though you bring me burnt offerings and grain offerings, I will not accept them. Though you bring choice fellowship offerings, I will have no regard for them. Away with the noise of your songs! I will not listen to the music of your harps. But let justice roll down like a river, righteousness like an ever flowing stream!' (Amos 4:21-24).

Members of a congregation were spending considerable time decorating their church for the occasion of the harvest thanksgiving. Many had brought gifts of flowers, fruit, vegetables and bread. One lady, who had recently started to attend the church, came with some fruit and asked if she could help in the decorating. She was given some flowers to arrange in a corner of the church. When she finished, some refreshment was being served and as she joined them she was distressed to hear what the other members were saying. They criticised the minister, questioned the honesty of the organist, complained about the choir and argued that the leaders should never have allowed a certain person to become a Lay Preacher because he had only joined the church four years ago. To make matters worse, when she turned around, the person who had asked her to arrange the flowers, was now re-arranging them in a different place! The following day the sanctuary looked beautiful and everyone remarked on the wonderful service, but what did the Lord see and hear?

Sometimes we may glimpse what the Lord is seeing. Have you watched a child working hard? Perhaps she is finishing a painting or drawing. You know she is concentrating because her tongue is pressing the outside of her lip! She ignores everything happening around her until the art work is finished. Then with pride the picture is presented and you tell her, 'It is lovely!' With obvious joy, she announces, 'It's for you!' What do you see? The lines which are not straight? The colours clashing with each other? The people who are out of proportion with the buildings? No. Surely what you see is the heart of generosity in a child who is giving her best, even if it is not a masterpiece. That is sacrifice; the giving of your very best, from your heart.

When Abel brought his lamb, the very first one to be born, his whole being must have screamed to protect and keep it. Yet he gave to God that which he most wanted for himself, and if the Lord would not accept his gift, Abel could not take it back. Cain, on the other hand, had brought the gift appropriate for a tillage farmer. The ancient Law of Israel required that when the first sprouts of grain appeared, they were to be plucked from the ground, before any harvest was assured and brought in a sheaf to be waved before the Lord (Lev 23). Then fifty days later, (which is the meaning of Pentecost) when the yearling lamb was sacrificed, the farmer would make bread from the fuller grain and all would be offered together to the Lord. When Cain brought his gift, he waved it half-heartedly before the Lord.

In a town on the west coast of Ireland is a memorial to the many men and women who left the country in poverty, to make a new life in America during the early 1800s. The memorial consists of the statue of a woman, dressed in the black cloak, waving towards a sailing ship, which has left the harbour and is disappearing from view. Like hundreds of her generation, she said farewell to a loved one whom she would never see again. What did her kinsman see from the deck of the ship? A raised hand dismissing him from memory or a heart, worn on the sleeve of her cloak, sighing for a reunion which would not happen? 'As the running deer pants for the water, so my soul yearns after you,' O Lord' (Ps 42:1). Cain's wave before the Lord lacked his heartfelt thanks for the harvest he'd been given or desire for closer friendship with God.

So, with what shall we come before the Lord, and what are the sacrifices of our worship? In what ways can we offer our whole selves as Paul instructs in the reading from Romans 12? It involves the sacrifice of our whole selves.

On moving to a new town, a friend and his wife went to several churches. After experiencing various styles of worship and being welcomed in many, his wife asked that they should join one where the style of worship was quite different from what they had previously been accustomed. He was reluctant. The praise was long and repetitive, and folk danced with the rhythm and he had no sense of timing. However, he agreed to give up his personal preference in order to accommodate his wife. In a few weeks, he found a new freedom in his personal life and actually enjoyed the praise of their new church. By setting aside his own desire so that others could come closer to God, he had made the willing sacrifice of praise and discovered God blessing him in unexpected ways.

Jesus has demanded that we are to be prepared to sacrifice our rights, in order to offer acceptable worship. Having done nothing wrong yourself, it may be that someone holds something against you. 'If so,' he said, 'leave your gift at the altar and go to seek reconciliation first.' Standing on our rights may rob us of the humility we need to walk with God. Jesus had no time for placing position and the dignity of a person's reputation before his service to his neighbour.

See him again in the Upper Room. Whilst his disciples argued about who was of greatest standing, Jesus himself took the towel and washed their feet.

When King David had similarly divested himself of his robe, in order to dance before the Ark of the Covenant, his wife Michal called him a vulgar fool (2 Sam 6:20). But God looked on David's exuberant heart and gave him honour. Often our usefulness to the Lord is in direct proportion to our willingness to be thought foolish. Didn't Paul refer to the foolishness of what we preach being the power of God? The Cross of Jesus was foolishness to the Gentiles because they put great importance on how things look.

Have we sacrificed our ambitions to the cause of the kingdom of God? An employer asked one man to use a legal loophole and deceive a partner in order to further his career. The man refused. As a result he was passed over for promotion many times, until the day he retired. On that day, many of his colleagues came to him, asking where he had got the courage to be honest and could they too find it in the God he served. He had lost much possible wealth, but kept peace at home and in his heart.

Our worship consists not only of the songs and prayers we sing or say. It is no single spiritual act, but a way of living which affects our hopes and dreams, our wealth and time, our relationships and the way we do our work. The prophet Micah pointed out what the Lord requires: that we 'act justly, love mercy and walk humbly with our God' (Mic 6:8). To live this way will mean becoming ever more dependent on God for grace and provision. And that requires that we trust him.

Prayer:
In praying we call to mind the sacrifice which is above all, made for us:

See from his head, his hands, his feet,
Sorrow and love flow mingled down.
Did e'er such love and sorrow meet?
Or thorns compose so rich a crown?

Were the whole realm of nature mine,
That were an offering far too small.
Love, so amazing, so divine
Demands my soul, my life, my all.
Isaac Watts

Eden's buried treasure
Building a vision of heaven on earth

Fergus Ryan

*A river watering the garden flowed from Eden; from there it was
separated into four headwaters. The name of the first is Pishon; it
winds through the entire land of Havilah, where there is gold. The gold
of that land is good; pearls and onyx are also there. Genesis 2:10-12*

Treasures of Egypt

Some time ago two archaeologists examining the Great Pyramid
near Cairo fell upon a startling discovery. A 200mm square shaft
running from the king's burial chamber to the outside and another from the queen's chamber had largely gone unnoticed as
they didn't have any obvious ritual significance. But by calculat-
ing the earth's position at the time of construction in 2450BC,
astronomers discovered that the shafts then pointed to a star in
the belt of the constellation Orion which represented the god
Osiris, and to the star Sirius which represented the god Isis. The
king and queen were 'locked onto' the principal gods of Egypt!
The archaeologists then stumbled upon the most astonishing
discovery of all. The entire pyramid complex was laid out as a
'map' of the stars of Orion, and was set in the same relative position to the River Nile on the earth as Orion is to the Milky Way
in the heavens. If these archaeologists are right, then what the
pagan Egyptians had attempted to do was nothing less than to
create heaven on earth!

God's heaven-on-earth society

Of course, God's plan has always been to create a heaven-on-
earth society, one living out the reality of the prayer 'Thy will be
done on earth as it is in heaven'. As servants of Christ we are
part of God's continuing strategy in history, co-workers with

him in calling out a people from every nation and envisioning them to be his beautiful 'city' set on a hill for all the world to see, a developing model and manifestation of what it is like when men and women live under the rule of God, and a pointer to its final great completion. In this 'city' with its 'temple' of living stones, God dwells on earth by his Spirit. All its people are, properly speaking, 'priests', who with one hand touch God and with the other touch those around them. The dynamic of its mission is not so much to get people to heaven when they die, as to bring something of heaven to people while they're still alive. Evangelism is less about escape, more about invasion. It's less about a 'gospel train' heading for heaven calling people to jump on; it's more like a train coming out of heaven with kingdom people jumping off, who are filling the earth with hope and healing. Jesus did not come to flee the works of the devil and abandon creation, he came to destroy them and to liberate creation from its bondage at the final revealing of the sons of God (1 Jn 3:8; Rom 8:21). The mission of the church is both a message about Jesus and his kingdom (Acts 28:30-31) and a manifestation of that kingdom through his redeemed people. It has to do with the binding up of broken hearts, the setting free of captives, the giving of a garment of praise instead of a spirit of despair (Is 61; Lk 4:18f).

Treasures of Eden

This heaven-on-earth society began in God's presence in Eden, where man and woman, made to bear the image of God, were appointed to fill the whole earth with image bearers and to exercise dominion as God's earthly regents. Earth's first rulers were, if we may say so, 'locked onto' their Creator and Lover and Lord. Notwithstanding the derailing of the process by sin, God was, and is still, determined to complete his great purpose of re-building his great universal 'city', once again filling the earth with his image and presence. This 'city' is the redeemed people the Father gives to his Son as a beautiful bride. The garden's features repeatedly appear in scripture as metaphors and symbols of God's grand plan: the Tree of Life (the wholeness and healing which comes from relationship with God), the river (the life-giving Spirit who refreshes us and quenches our thirst), the serpent (who repeatedly misaligns the signpost that says 'This way to the Garden of Delights').

But the treasures seem to have gone largely unnoticed: gold, pearls and precious stones (Gen 2:10-12). They too recur throughout scripture but, passing too quickly in the Genesis text, we have scarcely been prepared for the breathtaking vision of the use to which they have been put. As leaders it is our calling to help others see and be motivated by the vision of God's strategy for his new society. More often, however, we are just too busy with the routines of everyday church life to think about something as ephemeral as vision, and so, as Mark Twain said, having lost sight of our goal, we redouble our efforts! To put it another way, where the vision is unclear no one will ever pay the price to accomplish it. It's time we did a little digging in the garden.

A Tale of Two Cities

Early in salvation history, God determined to establish a model city. It would not be the real thing, so to speak, but a sample of the real thing. It was Jerusalem. Here God dwelt in his Temple amongst the people he had chosen to be his model society. The nation was built on the foundation of the twelve patriarchs and lived out the principles of God's government. The purpose of all this was that through the modelling of life under the true God, all the nations of the earth would be blessed. Amongst the nations of the world, Israel would be 'God's kingdom'. But there was a challenge to God from another city. It was Babylon, the people of which, following the advice of the Serpent, sought through building a tower (a ziggurat?) to take the place of God. Babylon symbolises the world in its opposition to God. It too is a model.

Israel however, did not 'live Jerusalem'; they rebelled and 'lived Babylon'. Hence, by making 'Babylon' choices, they ended up in captivity in Babylon itself. Instead of blessing the nations, they were ensnared by them. The Lord appeared to have deserted Zion. Isaiah foretold of the Lord's servant who would take the sins of Israel upon himself and spoke of the future glory of his city. 'O afflicted city ... I will build you with stones of turquoise, your foundations with sapphires. I will make your battlements of rubies, your gates of sparkling jewels and all your walls of precious stones' (Is 54:11-12). Were the symbolic treasures of Eden somehow to be used to rebuild and beautify Jerusalem? The Servant himself would later take the shadow world of the model city and its temple, and begin to build the real thing.

The Real Thing

Jesus began by announcing that the 'kinging' of God was at hand, and calling people to believe the good news about the kingdom (Mk 1:15). The Father's will was about to be demonstrated on the earth, and he would indeed return to Zion. It was not, however, Israel's political enemy that would be destroyed, but her spiritual captor. Jesus came to destroy the works of the devil. So having confronted Satan, Jesus announced a kingdom not of this world. Fulfilling the model, he established its new society on twelve new patriarchs, the twelve apostles. Later, when shown the beautiful buildings of the Temple, he announced that this 'joy of the whole earth' would be pulled apart stone by stone. The old Temple symbolised exclusion and religious privilege. Barrier after barrier excluded first the unclean, then the Gentiles, then the women, then the Israelite men, then the ordinary priests, and even, except for one day each year, the High Priest himself. Jesus, however, was building a new Temple. This one would be made up of living stones – Jews and Gentiles, male and female, slave and free, all of whom would have the religious privileges of the priests, since by Jesus' sacrifice he made the way into the Most Holy Place open to all who would come to the Father by him. In this Temple, too, would flow Eden's river, the promised Holy Spirit (Ezek 47; Jn 7:37-39). Whoever believed in Jesus, would continue, by the Spirit, to do the same kingdom ministry as he had done (Jn 14:12f). Jesus, of course, called Israel (the model) to be part of the real thing, but they crucified him for the offer.

Not only was Jesus, through his Spirit-filled people, building the new and everlasting kingdom (the real thing), and also building a new and everlasting Temple that will never be destroyed, he was building a new 'Jerusalem', the real city of God. Paul argues in Galatians 4 that it is not the present earthly city of Jerusalem that is our spiritual mother, but the Jerusalem that is above. The writer of Hebrews tells of a heavenly mount Zion, a New Jerusalem to which we have come (Heb 12:22). The old tabernacle, like the old nation, is 'a shadow of things to come'; the real thing is the new society which Jesus is building. Even Abraham was looking forward to this city, one with foundations whose architect and builder is God, for here we have no abiding city (Heb 11:10; 13:14).

And then – the wonder of it! – we are given in John's vision a revelation of God's completed work of redemption on the earth. 'New Jerusalem', coming to the earth from heaven as a bride adorned for her husband, has reached its full number. It is filled with '12s' – 12 thousand stadia long and wide and high (cubic, like the Holy of Holies), the walls are 144 (12x12) cubits thick, there are 12 foundations and 12 gates – the number symbolising the whole of God's people. The names of the 12 apostles are on its foundations, for it is built on them, and the names of Israel's 12 tribes are written over the gates, for many from the old Israel are amongst the redeemed. There is no Temple here, no death, no tears. And, as in Eden, the dwelling place of God is once again with men. The River of Eden flows from the throne of God, with the Tree of Life on its banks for the healing of the nations. (Rev 21, 22).These things are, as John said, signified to us – they are 'signs'; the final reality is beyond our present ability to grasp.

But wonder of wonders, the new Jerusalem is built from Eden's treasures, for its foundations are of precious stones, its streets of pure gold, and each of its gates a single pearl – the pearly gates! Even as I write, my breath is taken away by the

vision of it. It is not so much a picture of 'heaven', but of the new
society of the Bride and her Beloved living together in the final
fusion of heaven and earth.

And then the end will come
The worldwide church of Christ is the people of the coming
New Jerusalem, a city even now being formed by every kingdom action and comprised of every believer. Since we are already tasting 'the powers of the coming age' (Heb 6:5), Christian
mission involves bringing the blessings of the New Jerusalem
and displaying them in substantial measure on the earth now.
Some of these things are 'not yet' (we must not be unrealistic)
but some are 'already' (we must not have too little faith).
Though the 'end' is not yet, there may be a sense in which we
hasten its coming by the proclamation of the good news of Jesus
and the kingdom to the whole earth (Mt 24:14; 2 Pet 3:12).

But in the meantime our ministry as Christian leaders is to
seek (by releasing church members into their ministry as royal
priests) to demonstrate as much of heaven's 'nation' on earth as
we can (Rev 1:6). It is our goal (although painfully elusive at
times) that those who come in amongst us may experience the
manifest presence of God and say 'Surely God is among you!' (1
Cor 14:25; cf. Ex 33:15-16). If the NIV translation of Matthew
11:12 is the correct one, then we are to lay hold of the heavenly
kingdom forcefully, and by faith bring it into the lives of the
world's hurting people. The Jesus-type mission which has been
committed to our charge is taking what is in the Father's heavenly treasury, and in the power of the Spirit bringing it into the
loneliness and brokenness, injustice and powerlessness, despair
and depression, sickness and sadness, selfishness and sinfulness
that is all around us. Every deed done in Jesus' name is another
sparkling piece of gold and precious stones and pearls. Nothing
is lost. Every prodigal son who comes home to the Father is another piece of Jasper in the walls of the New Jerusalem.

It matters what we do. Our words and deeds build Jerusalem
or they build Babylon. Even when our 'Jesus-actions' seem with-

out obvious effect, the Lord 'will not forget your work and the love you have shown as you have helped his people and continue to help them' (Heb 6:10). Our labour in the Lord is not for nothing. The fire of God will test what lasts (the treasures) and what perishes (the trash). We may be assured that in the end Babylon will be destroyed, and Jerusalem, whose kingdom treasures we have built with, will last forever. Heaven will have come to earth.

Prayer
Father in heaven, I want your Name to be held in high esteem in all the earth. May your kingdom come into your church and into the world so that you rule in every part. I long to see your will displayed on the earth, where I live and work, just as it is in your very presence in heaven. Give me just what I need. Forgive me for sinning against you, and help me to share your forgiveness with others. Lord you know my frailties, so please keep me from traps of the devil, because the kingdom is rightfully yours, and you are powerful, and I long to see your glory displayed now and for ever. Amen.

'But what about you? Who do you say I am?'

Gillian Kingston

Matthew 16:13-19 (cf. Mark 8:27-30; Luke 9:18-21)
The Staff room at Break
'Come on, Gillian, you're the God person! What does this really mean? I've got a class after break,' and my colleague thrusts a poetry book between me and my hard-earned cup of a well-known brand of instant coffee and jabs her finger at a sonnet by John Donne. I read:

Batter my heart, three-person'd God, for you

As yet but knocke …

and I launch into a diffident explanation of the Trinity and a personal knowledge of God and temptation and repentance and forgiveness and all the other theological questions raised by that powerful poet in this particular sonnet.

'Well, if you say so,' she says, ' I don't believe any of that stuff at all!' This is a conversation we have often had, as there are so many Christian references in poetry of previous generations, and even of this generation. You don't get far with Shakespeare either if you don't know your Bible! And Patrick Kavanagh would be frequently incomprehensible!

What it all comes down to is what I think of the claims of one Jesus of Nazareth, called the Christ, who may well have been a historical figure, but can he possibly be of eternal significance? And anyway, who was he?

Pertinent questions
The scene is Caesarea Philippi, some miles north of Lake Galilee; formerly named after the Greek god, Pan, whose shrine had been there, it had been re-named by the Romans. In this place of three competing cultures, Greek, Roman and Jewish, Jesus of

Nazareth turns to the small band of men accompanying him and asks two straight questions, followed by a declaration concerning one of those men.

The synoptic gospel writers clearly considered this incident to be of such significance that each of them puts it on record. Chronologically, they place the incident between the feeding of many thousands of people at Lake Galilee and the Transfiguration, possibly on Mount Tabor. John does something slightly different, not unexpectedly (Jn 67-69). The issue, however, is the same for each of them: the identity of this strange and disturbing teacher and how he was perceived by those around him. Matthew, however, is alone in turning the spotlight on Peter as a future leader of the community of faith, a matter later to become a divisive issue among the churches.

The questions of one century, even of one millennium, are not necessarily those of the next and the issues of one time may be resolved by time itself. Of what relevance, then, is this little episode for Christians living two thousand years later?

'What about you? Who do you say that I am?'
Each of us, as an individual, needs to ponder on this question. Who is he …for me? Is he the Christ, the Son of the Living God, and, if he is, what are the implications of that for the way I live my life? Is his teaching and example the model for my life? And if he is not the Son of the Living God, then who is he and, in that case, can I go on calling myself a Christ-ian? This is a deeply personal and disturbing question.

In a time which puts a high premium on the freedom and ability to choose, to make exclusive claims about the nature of Jesus Christ, the only Son of God, appears to verge on the politically incorrect. There are many, even in the churches, who believe that we must allow for conscientious difference of opinion. He may be the Son of God for *me, my* Saviour, but that's it; I cannot, and should not, expect others to believe the same. A good man or the Christ of God? One among many or the Only Son?

On the other hand, such freedom of belief and expression

puts an onus on each of us to have 'a reason for the hope that is in us' (1 Pet 3:15). Others, like my friend, are interested in, even if sceptical of, what we believe, and they will have little time for the 'party line', it needs to be my line and your line. Who do you say that he is?

The implications for ministry are obvious: a priority must be teaching, coupled with the enabling of Christians to articulate the faith, 'faith sharing' as some call it. This is of course, important for all Christians in an increasingly secular society who frequently have to account for ourselves. Systematic courses of Bible teaching and discussion, such as the Emmaus or Alpha schemes, and Bible study leadership days, all contribute to the nurture of an articulate Christian community which can hold its own in the face of competing faith claims and in the vacuum of non-belief.

Who do people say the Son of Man is?
Who people say Jesus is depends to a considerable extent on who *we* say he is.

It has been said that most people come to faith in Jesus Christ through personal contact with individual Christians, rather than through giant rallies addressed by famous evangelists. This is both encouraging and terrifying! It is from us that they, whoever they are, hear. Indeed, as Paul observed to the Christians in the Rome of his time, 'How can they hear unless someone tells them?' (Rom 10:14). Mission and teaching/learning the faith are inextricably bound together.

Let me tell one of my favourite stories:
The monks of St Whatsit's had a custom of gathering in the chapel every morning for worship. One morning it was Brother Joe's turn to preach to his brother monks, so he mounted the pulpit and addressed them:
'Brothers, do you know what I am going to preach about this morning?'
'No, Brother Joe,' they replied, somewhat perplexed.
'Well, neither do I, so let's sing a hymn and go to breakfast!'

The Abbot was unamused, so Brother Joe was on the next day.

'Brothers,' he said, 'Do you know what I am going to preach about this morning?'

'Yes, Brother Joe,' they chorused knowingly.

'In that case, there is no need for me to tell you, so let's sing and go to breakfast!'

The Abbot was even less amused, so Brother Joe was in the pulpit the following morning too.

'Brothers,' he said, 'Do you know what I am going to preach about this morning?'

They were ready for this, so half of them said, 'Yes, Brother Joe,' while the other half said 'No, Brother Joe.'

'In that case,' he responded, 'Those of you who know must tell those who don't know: that is what the gospel is about.'

The Abbot knew when he had heard a good sermon!

Certainly those who know must tell those who do not know: that is the essence of gospel.

But 'gossiping the gospel' comes easily to only a few, for the rest of us it is an acquired art. And art it is to present the fundamentals of the faith in language and form that is attractive to a largely disinterested society.

Luke, recording the Pentecost story, notes that there were people from much of the then known world in Jerusalem for the feast. As they listened to this strangely excited bunch of Galileans, they suddenly realised that they were speaking in languages which could be understood (Acts 2:8): each was hearing about the Christ event in her/his own language.

Mission is about people hearing about Jesus Christ in terms they can understand, and that is now in the languages of the young, the deprived, the marginalised, the alienated, the abused, to name but a few. And we may have to 'offer Christ', as John Wesley put it, through the soundbyte, the internet and the entertainment industry.

'We hear them declaring the wonders of God in our own tongues!'

And again, the implications for ministry are obvious. Information technology has relevance to the sharing of the gospel, as other seemingly incongruous things, the Roman system of roads, for example, had in other times! What is equally obvious, however, is that the one who is perceived as being the 'official minister' cannot hope to be all things to all people simultaneously. A ministry which is 'to serve the present age' (*pace* Charles Wesley) is a ministry in which the whole community of faith shares, bringing into play the variety of areas of expertise which natural talent or training may have given each individual.

Questions of the third millennium

The first millennium may well have seen a relatively united church, existing in a political set-up where Christianity became the norm; the second millennium saw a church rapidly disintegrating, with an increasing number of challenges to its authority; the third millennium will almost certainly see a post-denominational church, in a world which couldn't care less one way or another. The individual, conscious of a spiritual vacuum, will be presented with the claims of many belief systems on a take-it-or-leave-it basis, where there will be many relativities and few absolutes. That is, of course, very sweeping and probably simplistic, but that's how it seems.

It is highly unlikely, for instance, that the issue of leadership in the church, which seems to have occupied the Matthean community and has certainly occupied and polarised Christians for centuries, will be the focus of attention in the third millennium. Circumstances will oblige Christians to relate more closely to each other. Jesus' prayer that we may be one that the world may believe will have to be taken seriously, whether we like it or not. The important questions will be those of the identity and significance of Jesus Christ himself.

The questions Jesus of Nazareth posed to his followers that day in Caesarea Philippi, a modern Roman city built on the site of a Greek shrine, are as relevant today as they were then. Who do people say I am? What about you? Who do you say that I am?

Back to school then, and to John Donne:
Batter my heart, three person'd God, for you
As yet but knocke…'

Prayer:
Gracious and Loving Father,
We thank you that, in your great love for us, you sent Jesus Christ, your only Son, to walk this life beside us.
We thank you that, through the power of the Holy Spirit, we can know him as Friend and Teacher.
Forgive us if we have taken this privilege for granted, and failed to communicate his presence to others.
Give us the grace and wisdom to spread the news of his love among all we meet and the strength and humility to witness to his name in all places and at all times.
We pray in his name and for his sake, Jesus Christ, our Lord.

Inviting commonality – the body of Christ

Sinclair Lewis

'Now you are the body of Christ and each one is a part of it.'
(1 Corinthians 12:27)

History and context vary but the plain, common task of the church is to portray Jesus. Philip spoke to Nathaniel and said 'come and see.' Christ's invitation to the first disciples was 'Come, follow me.' It was so utterly simple, without wordy arguments or high-sounding phrases. It was the invitation of one heart to another. It was like the invitation of a mother to a child, 'Come with me.' It was like the generous gesture across the religious divide by John Wesley who said 'if your heart is as my heart, give me your hand.' 'Come with me.'

In every congregation there is a commonality for we are always bonded in the body of Christ. Paul says: 'Now you are the body of Christ and individually members of it.' He starts with the word 'Now'. *Now* you are the body of Christ, the community of faith. It does not say you were so in the past and you have to recover the beautiful past. It doesn't say some day you will be if you try hard enough. It says 'this moment, right now, as you hear these words, you are the body of Christ'. God's work is for now or it is never done. It is not for the past or the future but for now.

To whom is this word addressed? It is addressed to you! It is not addressed to the United States or the world in general but it is God speaking personally to you and to me now. 'Now you are the body of Christ.' When Paul speaks to the church in Corinth he described what that little group was like. They were ordinary like us for 'not many of you are wise according to worldly standards, not many powerful, not many of noble birth'. The congregation was a weak minority assembled together in that great swarming city of Corinth. Today, as God speaks to you and me in our churches, no matter how large, we are still a weak minority made up of all sorts and conditions of people. We have not the money nor the battalions nor the votes to make anybody obey. Yet God speaks to all of us and says: 'You are the body of Christ.' God doesn't tell us that we ought to be the body of Christ. He says 'you are'. God does not tell us to strive to be the body of Christ. God has at some moment reached down from heaven and drafted us into his army. How strange that God in his almighty power decides to work through ordinary people like us. That's the way God chooses to work in his world. He wants people, so he calls us and enlists us. We can be AWOL (absent without leave), we can desert or we can regret that we were enlisted. We can make all sorts of responses but once he has laid his hand upon us there is no escape. Theologically we say once you are baptised you can't get 'unbaptised'. The Lord says to those gathered together in his name, 'I have called you, drafted you, you are part of my body, the community of faith.'

You understand what that means? When God fully revealed himself and let his love be unmistakably known on earth, he did it in human flesh, in the flesh of Jesus of Nazareth. People could touch Christ, hear him, yes they could spit on him and hang him upon a cross. God was embodied in Jesus. After he was crucified, dead and buried, he rose again and the spirit of the risen Christ was shared with the apostles and believers so that he could be embodied in them once again. Now God is embodied, not in one unique Jesus Christ but in ordinary men and women and children spread all over the face of the globe. To say that we are the body of Christ is to say that ordinary church members are the ones through whom God is going to move in this world. That's why every church, cathedral and chapel is built, to call people to be the ones through whom he can speak, through whom he can listen, through whom he can feed, heal, teach, and bring new light, life and joy into this world. The bottom line of the accounting for every local church will not be how many members we have nor how well-balanced is the budget nor how beautiful or functional are the buildings. The bottom line will be: were we or were we not Christ's body in our town? This is God's expectation for the church. That has to be our expectation for ourselves.

Dr Fred Craddock, in one of his sermons, tells a story about his first appointment. He and his wife were sent to a small mountain community in north Georgia. It was the custom of that local church that they baptise once a year and they did the baptisms in a small stream. On the day of the baptisms they gathered at the stream, built a fire, hung blankets to make a changing room. Dr Craddock, remembering that preachers were expendable, went into the water first, followed by those to be baptised and he baptised them. They then came back on dry land, went into the dressing room, and then came back to the fire. The elder patriarch of the congregation then called the name of one of the newly baptised. He introduced them to each of the members.

'Joe,' he said, 'this is George.' George responded with 'I run an auto repair service, if you need help with your car, call me.' 'Joe, this is Sara,' and Sara responded, 'I'm always available if you need a baby-sitter or just someone to talk with.' Around the circle they went … 'my name is' … 'if you need …' Dr Craddock then said they ate and danced and finally they covered the fire and went home. When Dr Craddock later told this story some-one asked, 'What did they call that thing that had happened down by the stream?' Dr Craddock answered, 'Why, they call that church, they call that church!' How beautifully they cared for each other in that small church.

While the truths of the gospel remain unchanged, God con-tinually calls us in new ways to re-engage the world as the body of Christ. We will be people of prayer who will reflect the light of his love in the world. As we do that, our life will be full and blessed and joyous, but not perfect nor without pain. So it was with the body of Christ. 'Now you are the body of Christ.'

Prayer:
Christ, from whom all blessings flow,
Perfecting the saints below,
Hear us, who thy nature share,
Who thy mystic body are.

Join us, in one spirit join,
Let us still receive of thine;
Still for more on thee we call,
Thou who fillest all in all.

Closer knit to thee, our Head,
Nourished, Lord, by thee, and fed,
Let us daily growth receive,
More in Jesus Christ believe.

Never from thy service move,
Needful to each other prove,
Use the grace on each bestowed,
Tempered by the art of God.

Love, like death, has all destroyed,
Rendered all distinctions void;
Names, and sects, and parties fall:
Thou, O Christ, art all in all.
Charles Wesley

Pattern and priority

John Faris

Mark 1:21-39
v 22 'the people were amazed at his teaching
because he taught them as one who had authority,
not as the teachers of the law.

People sometimes wish they had lived in the time of Jesus,
to walk with him, to hear his voice, to feel his touch.
Perhaps we can do that by using our imaginations
in a 'five senses' bible study.
It is not that difficult. We read a passage
and try to imagine the scene with our senses
as though we were there.
What do we see, hear, touch, taste, smell?

We find ourselves in the synagogue at Capernaum:
smell the polished wood, the dusty scrolls,
the scent of vegetation through the open door,
even the odour of human bodies squashed together.
Let's hear the voices at prayer, reading the scriptures,
the chanting of the cantor,
even the high-pitched wavering voice of a scholarly scribe:
'Rabbi X says this, Rabbi Y says that,
on the one hand, on the other ...'
Look around at the eyes of people glazing over, trying to listen,
stifling yawns, trying to stop the children fidget.

And then a different voice cuts through,
probably quietly and gently
but with the unmistakable tone of one who knows
who speaks with authority.

v 22 'the people were amazed at his teaching
because he taught them as one who had authority,
not as the teachers of the law.
So much religion is words *about* God: Jesus spoke words *from* God.
No dithering, no waffling,
he spoke with complete personal security,
complete certainty from a personal knowledge
of God his Father.
That is something we all want to hear when a preacher speaks:
a clear word from God.
Something you need to pray for the preacher
that the Spirit will give the clear word of Christ.
'We do not have to make any secret of our preacher's fallibility
or of our own spiritual deafness.
but we know that, still, when Sunday comes
Christ goes into the church and teaches.
We gather with expectation
because we believe he can and will take up
the preacher's stumbling words into his own service
and enable us to hear through them his own word to us.
And when that happens
we are no longer left with mere opinions
which we can listen to or ignore as we please.
When Christ speaks to us he tells us the truth about our lives,
truth that goes home, truth that commits.' *(James Leitch)*
Truth with authority is what we pray from every preacher.

What's all that shouting about?
Harsh screeching and roaring
from a man tormented by a demon.
How distressing and embarrassing
but that is what happens when the authority of Jesus
challenges an evil spirit.
This is not an intellectual seminar on the theology of evil;
this is a power encounter on a very deep level
which most of us, thankfully, rarely have to deal with.
But Jesus who is indeed the Holy One of God

has authority and power
to deal with every manifestation of evil.
Note that there were no arguments, no incantations,
no elaborate wrestling in prayer or rituals.
The spirit that was in Jesus
was more than equal to the evil spirit.
It is good to remember when we are downcast by great evil
that there is such power in the name of Jesus Christ.
Greater is he that is in you than he that is in the world. (1 Jn 4:4)

The service is over
and it is time for lunch at Simon Peter's house.
Just imagine the smell of cooking, the table spread for guests.
Doesn't your mouth water in anticipation?
But we see no smiles of welcome, instead frowns of worry.
Simon's mother in law is sick, tossing and turning with a fever.
What will Jesus do now?
Look carefully as he goes to her,
takes her hand and helps her up.
She's better! She's well enough to help with the dinner!
No wonder, that night, once the Sabbath is over,
that people flock round
and Jesus heals the sick and casts out more demons.
Can you sense the whispers in the crowd,
the shouts of delight of people healed, the murmurs of wonder,
the quiet firm voice of Jesus silencing the evil spirits?
At last the people leave, the household is tired, they lie down
and soon are fast asleep.
But very early in the morning, while it is still dark,
you can hear soft footsteps and a door creaking.
Someone has got up and gone out
and is walking out of the village.
Do you hear his footsteps receding
as a dog barks and a cock crows?
It is Jesus, gone to pray by himself
in the quiet of the very early morning.

Now we can begin to guess
at the reason for these amazing things:
Jesus keeps in touch with his heavenly Father.
He is never too busy to pray;
instead, when he is busy, prayer is a priority,
even more than ever.
Perhaps the events of the day before, so early in his ministry
require time for talking through with his Father.
Does he need to assess what priority he should give
to each aspect, to teaching, to healing, to driving out evil spirits?
Amid all the demands of people
he needs to hear what his Father says.

Oh dear, here come the practical disciples
stumbling and panting, scattering stones as they look for him.
Hear the tone of annoyance: *Everyone is looking for you.*
You can't just slip off like this, Jesus, when there's work to do.
Listen to the quiet answer of someone
who has been speaking with his Father:
Let us go somewhere else, to the nearby villages,
so that I can preach there also.
That is why I have come.
Through time given to prayer, time with his Father,
Jesus has reaffirmed his priority.
The healings and the other miracles are good,
they help people and they point to his divine nature.
But the good must never replace the best
which is to proclaim the kingdom of God at hand,
calling people to repent and to believe the good news.
And the best is also to move on in a journey which will climax
on a scaffold in Jerusalem.
And the best is seen as we sometimes sing:
'From the cross to the grave, from the grave to the sky ...'
for the risen Lord will open the kingdom of heaven
to all believers.
That is why Jesus has silenced the evil spirits;
his time has not yet come for being fully disclosed,

his 'best' is not served by becoming a spectacular healer.
That is why
although miraculous healing may still be a possibility today
(with God all things are possible)
in God's kingdom healing is not the priority.
The priority is to proclaim Jesus Christ and his kingdom.

Have we a true sense of priority in our lives,
individually and for the church?
Do we keep before us the underlying aim
so that not even the good will undermine the best?
Do we spend enough time,
perhaps especially in the early mornings
just talking to God the Father
about how things have been with us
and where we should be aiming and what he wants us to do?
All right then, if you are more of a 'night owl' than a 'sky lark',
and you function more brightly
late at night than in the early morning,
then use whatever time of day or night when you are most alert
and when there is space made to be alone with the Father.

If we spent more time with God the Father,
genuinely in his presence and not just rattling off a few prayers,
then would we not hear the voice of Christ
speaking with authority
and would we not sense more of his healing touch
and victory over evil
and see his pattern and priority for our lives?

Prayer:

Lord,
We have sought to go back to the days
when you were physically present in Galilee,
when people heard your voice and felt your loving touch;
we have sought to identify with the people of those days
weak and vulnerable as we also are,
needing you as we also need you.
By your Spirit may we hear Christ speaking with authority
so that as well as what we hear and see
and touch and taste and smell
we shall have a spiritual sense and discernment for your will.

'In the stillness of the morning
may your voice alone be heard.
In the quietness of your presence
may we hear your living word.
In the oneness of the Spirit
we would wait upon you, Lord.
In the stillness of the morning
may your blessing be outpoured.'

Called to encourage

Brian Callan

'Whatever is true, whatever is noble, whatever is right, whatever is pure, whatever is lovely, whatever is admirable – if anything is excellent or praiseworthy – think about such things.' Philippians 4:8

Encouragement is a gift

A famous singer was due to appear in a Paris Opera House. Tickets were sold out and the house was full to capacity on the night. There was an atmosphere of expectation throughout the theatre. The Opera House manager stepped onto the stage to announce that the singer had been involved in an accident, not serious, but would be unable to appear on the night. He went on to give the name of the understudy for the night but the groan of the disappointed crowd drowned him out. The stand-in singer gave the performance all he had but throughout the evening there was nothing but an uneasy silence and in the end no one applauded. Then from the balcony, a little girl's voice broke the silence. She shouted 'Daddy, I think you were wonderful.' The crowd broke into spontaneous and prolonged applause. That's the definition of encouragement that means most to me, 'Daddy, I think you're wonderful.'

Now reverse the picture and imagine the little girl on stage, standing all alone in silence and the father wanting to reach out, straining to reach out and gather the little girl into his arms and there you have the picture of God wanting to reach out to his children. The Bible is a book of promises. It is the mission of God to the world to say he cares about us, not that he needs us, but that he wants us. The Bible is essentially a love story, and many of the promises contained in it are an encouragement to those who seek after God. As well as the promises of God, the Bible also outlines a series of gifts bestowed by God, such as those contained in Romans 12:6-8, namely prophecy, serving, teaching, encouraging, giving leadership and showing mercy. There is another list in 1 Corinthians 12, which talks of gifts God has given to the church; these include miracles, healing, speaking in tongues and interpretation of tongues. Sadly, a lot of people debate and fall out over interpretation of some of these more spectacular gifts whereas people seldom debate the gifts of encouraging, of serving or of helping. The focus of this chapter is on the gift of encouragement. The reasons I put forward for exploring the topic are, first that it is a gift, second that it is a very spiritual gift, and third that it is a gift that we and the church really need. I believe it is encouragement that will make us powerfully different as a church and more able to worship so that God will be glorified.

Encouragement is outreach

Our lives are made up of many intersecting circles of people, all of whom benefit from our conscious or unconscious encouragement. My wife, Jan and I recently watched a BBC documentary on depression and the presenter stated that 20% of people in the waiting rooms of UK doctors suffer from depression. That's a lot of people. I work as a chemist for a large multinational pharmaceutical firm and one of our biggest selling drugs is for depression and sales are growing enormously. If you apply the UK figures into any meeting of worship or gathering of people, the figures suggest that there are a lot of people having a very hard time. Depression is not like having your arm in a sling or your leg in a cast; it can be completely invisible but very painful. The real question is, are we as a church helping or hindering this hurt in those with whom we worship, and do we extend this to neighbours? The practical application of the gift of encouragement is to recognise those we live, work or worship with, who need to be encouraged. Everyone needs encouragement, whether we are in pain or not and encouragement is not just something that goes on around us, it's something we are part of. God wants to encourage his children, that's who we are, and he uses his children to do this, that's who we are. For those of us with children, there is the very useful challenge of 'catching them doing something right', that we might encourage by praise. Maybe your neighbour needs encouragement, even the grumpy one. Grumpiness can often be the outside face of loneliness or pain. Maybe the lady at the supermarket till needs encouragement. A smile goes a long way.

Encouragement is appreciation

Each year's Oscar nominations in March remind me of one interview that has always inspired me. This was given by the actress Meryl Streep. When she was asked a few years ago about her dreams of a third Oscar, her reply was a challenge: 'I'd rather be voted "mother of the year" by my family, because nobody realises that being a good mother is much harder than making a movie. Being a housewife and a mother is much more difficult.' One of the reasons I think this is a difficult job is that it doesn't get the acknowledgement and appreciation that it deserves. Hold these two words in your mind, acknowledgement and appreciation; these are key elements of the very simple gift of encouragement.

Psychologists say that if you ask people to write down on a piece of paper all their personality strengths, they will come up with a list of five or six. However, if you ask them to write a list of their weaknesses, the list will be three or four times longer. That's one of the reasons we need encouragement. It is sometimes only when other people notice what we do that it takes on any worth. Cooking the dinner would be a very different task, if the cook felt that those eating it were really appreciative.

Mother Teresa once said 'Being unwanted, unloved, uncared for, forgotten by everybody is a much greater hunger, a much greater poverty than the person who has nothing to eat.' Mother Teresa was famous for her kindness, often giving homes to the destitute of Calcutta, so they could die with some dignity but also feeling cared for. The challenge of Calcutta is equally the challenge of the Western church. How many people feel it doesn't matter if they come to church – who would miss them anyway? The person who really needs a word of encouragement may be the person we sit beside most Sundays, it may be the person whose best friend has gone on to heaven or it may be an exhausted mother. The parable of the talents told in Matthew 25:14-30, challenges us to use the gifts God has given us. In this context, you may be the person God has chosen to listen, to smile, to care for some particular person today. Caring is one of the core values of church life. We need to be a people who pick up the phone because someone has been missing for a while – maybe that someone needs us or needs to know that we are at least thinking about them. So kindness and caring are two more weapons in the war of encouragement. If the Holy Spirit brings a person into your mind, don't bury the thought, invest the thought in a phone call or a note in the post.

We have all been discouraged. There is a story told that one day the devil decided to go out of business and he wanted to sell all his tools to whoever would pay most for them. On the night of the sale, they were all attractively displayed. Malice, hate, envy, jealousy, greed, sensuality and deceit were among them. Also on the table was a harmless wedge-shaped tool, which had been used much more than any of the rest. Someone asked the devil, 'What is that? Why does it cost so much?' The devil answered, 'That's discouragement. The reason it is priced so much higher than the rest is because with this tool I can pry open and get inside a person's conscientiousness when I couldn't get near with any of the others. Once discouragement gets inside, I can let all the other tools do their work.' This is another excellent reason why we need to encourage. There is a whole world queuing up to discourage, to gossip, to feed on the negative.

Encouragement is a mind-set
The gift of encouragement is in many ways an attitude. It's where you thank total strangers on the way to work with a nod of the head, a thank-you glance, when they stop to let you into the traffic lane or when someone holds a door for you.

Encouragement may be as simple as a smile that says 'I'm happy to see you.' A few years ago a lady called Vera Wellcome came to worship in our church, but long before this I knew who she was. She was the lady who worked on the top floor in one of the major bookstores in the city I live in, who always smiled and for whom nothing was too much trouble. I didn't know her but I knew she had a gift, so much so, you watched her dealing with other customers because it made you feel good.

The first verse from Romans 12 tells us to be transformed by the renewing of our minds – this is our attitude. My best definition of attitude is also a story, told about a traveller nearing a great city who meets an old man seated by the wayside and he asks 'What are the people like in the city?' The old man replied with his own question, 'How were the people where you come from?' 'A terrible lot,' responded the traveller, 'Mean, untrustworthy, detestable in all respects.' 'Ah,' said the old man, 'You will find them the same in the city ahead.' Scarcely had the first traveller gone when another arrived, and he also inquired of the people in the city before him. Again the old man asked about the people in the city that the traveller had left. 'They were a fine people, honest, industrious and generous to a fault. I was sorry to leave,' declared the second traveller. The old man then said, 'You will find the people in the city ahead are very much the same as those in the city you left.' Attitude is what we take with us wherever we go, and it colours all we see and do. We can be positive and encourage or negative and discourage. Staying neutral, doing or saying nothing, can be just the same as discouraging because it says you don't care enough. Think of the person who annoys you most and look for something good about them; maybe your gift to Jesus should be to find some small way to encourage them.

Encouragement is love
To encourage literally means 'to put courage in' and it has the sense of telling someone 'You can do it, go for it.' When our daughter Michelle was five, we bought her a kite and it was one

of those magic investments. I remember being on a beach with her and she was flying the kite, not her mother or I, but Michelle. You had to see her face to appreciate it. Encouragement was making her believe she could do it and not being concerned if she smashed the kite in her attempts. You can do it.

When I was fourteen, my chemistry teacher at the technical school in Dundalk said to me one day, 'Brian, you could go to university,' and that statement probably shaped the rest of my life. Nobody from my very large extended family had ever gone to university. Nobody from the street where I grew up had ever gone to university, and I was the first student ever from my school to graduate from university. That may be because one teacher on one day said 'Brian, you could go to university.'

Some years ago, an American professor gave a group of graduate students an assignment to go into a poor area of town, to take 200 boys between the ages of twelve and sixteen, to investigate their background and environment and to predict their chances for the future. The study was completed and the end result was the prediction that 90% of the boys would spend some time in jail. Twenty-five years later another group of graduate students were given the job of testing the prediction. They managed to get in touch with 180 out of the original 200 but only 4 had ever been to jail. The researchers worked hard on this surprising record and kept coming up with the statement 'Well, there was a teacher …' In 75% of the cases the teacher was the same one and the researchers tracked her down to a retirement home and interviewed her. They wanted to know how she had exerted such a remarkable influence and all she could tell them was that 'I didn't do anything special, I just loved those boys.'

Decision

Like many gifts, exercising the gift is similar to going on a diet. You make the decision, you work hard at it until it becomes a habit and then it carries on by itself. But the important first step is making the decision, 'I'm going to do this. I am going to encourage someone today.' Anne Frank in her diary said 'It's wonderful that nobody needs to wait a single moment before start-ing to improve the world.' Encouragement is about appreciation, acknowledgement, caring, kindness, attitude and love. The lady who started Weight Watchers is called Jean Nidetch and, in an interview, she was asked how she was able to help so many peo-ple. She said that as a teenager she used to walk in the park and would see many mothers watchfully ignoring their children as the kids sat on the swings with no one to push them. She would go up and push the kids on the swing and pretty soon they would be pumping, doing it themselves. 'That's my rule in life,' she said, 'I'm there to give others a push.' What a great rule and what a good definition of encouragement, push for the positive.

A last word on gifts is borrowed from the biography of 'Holifield, The Humble Warrior.' He is a former heavyweight boxing champion. He grew up in a Christian home and de-scribes how his grandmother warned him about developing his gifts. She would say 'God didn't give you all these gifts so you could sit on them and be lazy. He gives you the gifts but it's up to you to do the polishing. And everyday that you don't polish your talent, you lose a piece of it.' Isn't that the parable of Jesus in a nutshell? Encouragement is a gift from God. It's about ap-preciation, acknowledgement, caring, kindness, attitude and love. 'Whatever is true, whatever is noble, whatever is right, whatever is pure, whatever is lovely, whatever is admirable – if anything is excellent or praiseworthy – think about such things' (Phil 4:8).

Prayer:
Lord, open our minds, make us aware of those you have placed within our reach, especially those who are hurting, discouraged and feel lost in a busy world. Lord, open our hearts with a sensitivity that feels the prompt of your Spirit to reach out in eager love. Use me today to help someone on their pilgrim journey from earth to glory, for the sake of Jesus Christ our Saviour. Amen.

A story for children

Lynda Neilands

Once upon a time there was a traveller – we'll call him Christian – who used his Bible as a guide in life. He read it as he rode his donkey through the countryside, with a cloak on his back, a sword at his side and a bag of gold in his pocket. Then one day a terrible storm blew up. The wind howled and the thunder crashed and suddenly Christian was stopped by a beggar. 'The wind has blown away my blanket!' the beggar yelled. 'You're a Christian. It's your duty to help.' Christian read from his Bible. Then he took off his cloak. 'Here, my friend, have this to keep you warm,' he said and hurried on his way.

A little further on he was stopped by a farmer. 'Lightening has just struck my barn,' the farmer yelled. 'You're a Christian. It's your duty to help.' Again Christian read from his Bible. Then he handed over his bag of gold. 'Here, my friend, take this and build a new barn,' he said and hurried on his way.

A little further down the road he was stopped by a fellow-traveller. 'My horse has broken its leg,' he said. 'You're a Christian. You should give me your donkey to make up.' Once again Christian read from his Bible, and this time he shook his head. 'I can't give you my means of transport,' he said. 'But here, take my sword, sell it and buy a new horse.'

He journeyed on and the donkey began to bray. 'I don't understand you, master,' it brayed. 'Those people were rude and undeserving, yet you've given them your possessions and left yourself defenceless. That Bible makes you act like a fool.'

Christian smiled and patted the donkey's shoulder. 'No, donkey,' he said. 'This Bible promises me a great inheritance. It says that all I have to do is reach the castle, where my father is

waiting to make me ruler of this land. It tells me I own
wardrobes full of cloaks and treasuries full of gold, and have
whole armies to defend me. This Bible doesn't make me act like
a fool. It teaches me to live like a Son.'

Every Christian ministers to someone

Cherie Ritchie

'All of you are Christ's body.'
1 Corinthians 12:27; 1 Corinthians 12 and 13

'Christian Ministry' – what reaction do these two words create in you?

Ministry – a minister as 'an executive agent' was a helpful description, indicating one who ministers to people, who does something for them, who is in contact with them. Ministry is more than witnessing. We speak of witnessing to people about what Jesus is doing in our lives; ministry is more dynamic, where something is transferred from one to the other.

Christian – this is the big challenge for us in our society today. Many fine people are following the way Christians have led over the centuries and are doing all kinds of good works. So is there a special Christian ministry? I think there is.

The Christian views a person as God's creation, a unique individual, valuable to him. So Christian ministry needs to be to the whole person, physical, emotional and spiritual, as to the one whom God created to be in his likeness, perfect and complete.

The other wonderful truth is that the one who ministers has the direction, as well as the seal, power, wisdom and love of God. His/her motive is to obey God and to work through the Holy Spirit in love and care for the other person. Above all, when a Christian ministers to another we believe that they and their situation can be changed by the power of God, and it is very exciting to see how God does work.

Does every Christian take part in Christian Ministry? Jesus calls all of us to follow him and to bring others to know him, 'to go to all people everywhere and make them my disciples' (Mt 28:18-20). Those who are in leadership in our churches have a special responsibility to encourage all to use their lives in full-time Christian ministry. Through our ordinary working lives, with the stresses, strains and opportunities, Christians so follow Jesus that everything we do is ministry for him. Take the teacher who has in her class a young boy whose grandmother has died recently. The young mother is very upset, so much so that her little boy says to her 'Mummy, why don't you talk to Jesus about it, my teacher says Jesus will help us when we are sad.' The woman finds an opportunity to talk to the teacher about this and, after several chats and prayer, joins an Alpha course. During this time she has a special experience of Christ which changes her life.

Every Christian ministers to someone, the people at work, the family, the neighbours, but what does this mean? Making them listen as we preach to them? It is rather a daily waiting on God for him to give us opportunities to share his love by our actions and by our words. It is interesting that in the preaching ministry particularly it is often not the sermons that mean most to people but the caring phone-call or the brief personal word that ministers Christ to them. In today's society, where more and more people have no church connections, we are finding that young and middle-aged are asking Christians whom they know, questions such as 'What is a real Christian? Why do you behave like that in work? How does a Christian parent deal with such and such a problem? What does your church say about this? Is church not boring and irrelevant?' Under God we are there to tell them that God loves them and wants to give to them 'life in all its fullness' (Jn 10:10). We can tell them of the difference a relationship with God through Jesus Christ would make to them because of our own experience. This of course challenges us as to whether our relationship with him is up to date, a daily experience. Sometimes I try to grow seed which is no good and it doesn't sprout, it's too old and is no longer alive. Sometimes our Christian witness is no longer alive, no longer relevant and therefore cannot bear fruit, 'some 100, or 60 or 30 fold' (Mt 13:23).

Christian Ministry is to all: the individual, the family, the community, our country and to the world. Each of us is called by God to minister in one or more of these areas and nowadays this will mean more and more frequently leaving our church buildings in order to be where people are. We minister by our behaviour, actions and attitudes, with our words, our love to others. Our basic belief is that Christ loves all, that he died for us to open up for us a new way of life in relationship with God and that he lives within us by the power of the Holy Spirit so that we can become like him and find and fulfil the purpose for which he caused us to be born.

What are the issues to which we need to pay special attention with different types of ministry both now and in the years ahead? Everyone will have different priorities, I list a few.

The absolute need of every man, women, boy and girl to hear of God's love shown through Jesus for them and to be given an opportunity to respond to it and to grow in faith. Our churches must provide teaching that will help people to grow in their faith on a daily basis. People need encouragement that will help them to minister to others. People need help and companionship when they are finding the going hard. Church must be a place where people share with each other the realities of their faith, find out that prayer matters, that worship is a real communion with God who speaks to us through Christ his living Word and written revelation in the Bible.

Missionaries have gone from Ireland to other lands and the whole Irish church has been enriched. Today we have thousands of visitors from other countries living and working among us and we are called to minister Christ to them. It may be their only opportunity of observing a true follower of Jesus or of visiting a Christian home or of seeing a Christian at work in their job. Is there anything significantly Christian about our ministry in these situations? Christians, following their Lord, stand for social and economic justice throughout our world. This can best happen when there is peace. Throughout the Old Testament we see prayers for peace that God's people may prosper, e.g. Psalm 122 v 6. Christ calls us to be peacemakers and Christians in Ireland are called to be ministers of peace. One of the terrible things about our Christian heritage is the way it has divided people. Can you imagine anyone wanting to join a church where the members are at odds with each other and critical of each other, where they won't associate with or trust Christians from other churches? In our contacts with Christians from other churches, have we ever had the joy of catching a fresh insight into the character of God or discovered some custom or practice that enriched our faith? Do we feel humbled when we see others thirsting to know more about Jesus, avidly reading the Bible to learn more? Are we ashamed that we have not shared our own experiences more when we see the joy with which people discover new ways of prayer? Christians are one body and we must minister and witness together to our Christian faith.

What about the way in which we treat others who are different from us in some way? They may be smaller, fatter, differently gifted or abled, those from different cultures, faiths, financial categories, of a different age or gender. When we meet someone, are we inclined to categorise them? Do we judge them by their outward appearance and discriminate because of our false judgements? Can we see God's hand at work in diversity and difference and be enriched by this? Take age for example; I read recently of the pastor who prayed every day that God would send them some older people to add experience and balance to their thriving congregation. Do we appreciate the unique gifts that our young people bring with enthusiasm and vision, and do we listen to what they are saying? This century has seen tremendous changes in the way in which women can take their place in our world. Some churches have a good record of opening all positions to women and men, but there are many places where women and children are badly treated and exploited and not allowed any say in their own destiny. Are we taking seriously the violence of all kinds to women and children? It is part of our ministry that we offer all persons the same recognition that Jesus did, and encourage others to do the same.

There is a Christian ministry to those who are consumed by fear and to those afraid of ill health, of death, or of failure in their working life or in their relationships. Christ ministers to all of us in these situations and he uses us to be his agents. Fears are much more active in the darkness of the night and so they are in the darkness of spiritual night for those who walk in darkness and do not have God's light, the presence of Jesus in their lives (1 Jn 1:7).

Are we ready and equipped to minister in the name of Jesus to all those who are searching and battling in life? Our attitudes to political, economic and social issues, the way we use our money, our attitude to material things, all must submit to the Lordship of Christ. What are our priorities as Christians, what is important to us? These daily decisions are a strong witness to our fellow humans about how important Christ is to us. We can minister Christ to others through sharing our priorities, the things that come up in everyday conversation and in the decisions we all have to take.

New technology issues a challenge and opportunity to the churches. Attitudes to leisure and work offer different opportunities to minister to homes where both parents work, or work alone from home. Those taking early retirement have opportunities for Christian service. I have not mentioned specifically ministry to children, young adults, singles, marrieds, senior citizens and many others. Where is God leading you to minister?

All Christians are ministers of Christ and need to be led by God to use the gifts of the Spirit. We see those to whom God has given gifts of teaching, preaching, hospitality and others, and yet the whole area of the gifts of the Spirit is part of our faith which has either been neglected or abused. We neglect these gifts of God at our peril. We limit the power and love of God if we do not allow him to lead us in his way which will bring honour and glory to him. Let us take very seriously all the teaching in 1 Corinthians chapters 12-14, that we may see his involvement in his world as our daily experience. Christian Ministry is possible when the fruit of the Spirit is evident, when a person is ministering by the gifts of the Spirit and realises that Christ's body is made up of many parts, each with a different function which is used to build up the whole.

Christian Ministry follows the pattern of the ministry of Jesus the suffering servant. We are called to take humbly the way of the cross for us, and not to look for recognition, praise or any reward 'save that of knowing we do God's will.' The Christian life lived with God in prayer, led and empowered by the Holy Spirit, is a Christian ministry. May we all be lost in wonder, love and praise as we seek to minister in, for and with Christ.

Prayer:

1 May the mind of Christ my Saviour
  Live in me from day to day,
  By his love and power controlling
  All I do or say.

2 May the word of God dwell richly
  In my heart from hour to hour,
  So that all may see I triumph
  Only through his power.

3 May the peace of God my Father
  Rule my life in everything,
  That I may be calm to comfort
  Sick and sorrowing.

4 May the love of Jesus fill me,
  As the waters fill the sea;
  Him exalting, self abasing –
  This is victory.

5 May I run the race before me,
  Strong and brave to face the foe,
  Looking only unto Jesus
  As I onward go.
  Kate Barclay Wilkinson (1859-1928)

Scriptural Holiness:
The not-so-hidden component
of Christian discipleship

Osmond Mulligan

*'But just as he who called you is holy, so be holy in all you do;
for it is written: Be holy, because I am holy.' 1 Peter 1:15-16.*

Mention of holiness produces a sinking feeling. It is so often associated with narrow-minded, unpractical, or other-worldly people. The people who were most interested in this subject during Jesus' lifetime were the Pharisees. They certainly weren't pleased with how Jesus, the Son of God, conducted himself. Today, there are similar groups of intense Christians who need to beware of modern Phariseeism. For too long this has been tolerated in some Christian circles. After all didn't Jesus, the perfect 'holiness' role model, enjoy the reputation of being 'the friend of sinners'? We need to rediscover how the modern church can model a contemporary, relevant, attractive and fruitful lifestyle. Without holiness it is impossible to please the Lord or to convince a cynical world that God is alive within his church.

At the British Methodist Conference in 1763, John Wesley initiated a question and answer session which was repeated annually until his death. It sought to clarify that Methodism was raised up 'to reform the church and nation – and to preach scriptural holiness across the land'. Holiness preaching, often referred to as Perfect Love, was central to the biblical message and had relevance for the everyone inside and outside the church.

Holiness is practical. An example of practical holiness comes from 'Habitat for Humanity', which is an organisation committed to providing housing for the most needy throughout the world, especially in countries which have experienced earthquake, tornado, hurricane and civil war. This organisation came to Northern Ireland where in 30 years of civil commotion homes and communities have been destroyed. Protection rackets by paramilitaries on housing sites had put up the cost of buildings. So Christians had the opportunity to cross social and cultural barriers and become physically involved in building affordable houses in two projects in Catholic and Protestant West Belfast. This was holiness in action and made a practical Christian and visible statement about justice and love. John Wesley taught his early followers that it was not enough to experience forgiveness of sins through saving faith in Jesus' atoning death. He encouraged people to display love, the fruit of the indwelling Spirit of God (1 Cor 13). We need to express this love.

Holiness demands reality. John Wesley contended for realism. In his day, as in ours, there were theologians who focused on one truth in scripture to the exclusion of another. The Pauline epistles clearly taught that the Christian only stands accepted in God's holy presence on the basis of the perfect sacrifice of Christ in atonement for our sins. We are accepted in Christ and not because of our achievements nor even because of the faith by which we appropriate his offer of forgiveness. On the day of final judgement we can only plead the merits of Jesus' perfect life for acceptance into God's holy heaven. Stated pictorially, when we all stand on the day of judgement, only those sinners covered by the coat of Christ's goodness will be allowed into God's heaven. Some people had so pushed the logic of this theology that they argued that we could keep on sinning (breaking God's perfect law) because God would have to pour out more grace and thus display his long-suffering and mercy (Rom 6:1ff). It was against this antinomianism that early Methodists preached. They emphasised that Jesus came to destroy the works of the devil. All sin, manifest in its power, guilt, or corruption, is the work of the devil. They believed that those who had experienced the grace of God would evidence the work of God within their lives by living a holy life like their Lord and could experience 'all the fullness of God' (Eph 3:19). Their focus was stimulated by the first epistle of John and the gospel of John. Such

verses as 1 Jn 2:1 which say 'I write this to you so that you will
not sin', or 1 Jn 3:6, 'No one who lives in him keeps on sinning.
No one who continues to sin has either seen him or known him.'
For Wesleyans the fruit of faith in Jesus Christ was love of God
and neighbour. The reality of a confession of Jesus as Lord and
Saviour was subject to an examination of behaviour, since 'Faith
without works is dead' (Jas 2:14-17).

The quotation in our text comes from the Leviticus 11:44,
which mentions the word 'holy' more often than any other book
of the Bible. The idea of 'holy' essentially conveyed the idea of
separateness, of being special. God is uniquely holy. He allowed
articles, people and places to be set aside for his purposes. They
too were called 'holy'.

But this text makes the point that we are to 'be' holy, not just
to 'act the part'. The emphasis is on 'being' as borne out by
Psalm 24:3ff: 'He who has clean hands and a pure heart, who
does not lift up his soul to what is false and does not swear de-
ceitfully.'

John Wesley knew that theory or theology did not always
match up with experience for many people. There was a desire
to live up to a certain standard when people became Christians,
but many found that desire and experience did not match up.
They recalled from scripture that the apostle Paul in Romans
chapter 7 spoke of his wretchedness at not being able to do the
things he wanted to do. Wesley did not believe that this was a
description of a 'man in Christ' but argued that it described the
experience of Paul as a religious man, under law, before conversion. Ever since then, bible scholars have debated this issue.
Many good Christians have been depressed by the experience of
defeat in their discipleship and see in Romans 7 a reflection of
their normal life. Wesley re-emphasised that in Romans 8:2 we
have the promise of the indwelling Holy Spirit to give us victory
over the law of sin and death to which we are all naturally heirs.
As sons and daughters of God, we have a new Spirit and are able
to overcome the 'natural' attractions of sin to which our bodies
and intellects so readily respond through the inherited habits of

innumerable generations since Adam. Indeed the theologians of earlier centuries called this tendency variously 'the old Adam', 'the old man', or 'inbred sin'. Wesley believed this principle could be overcome, through faith in a full atonement.

However, this became the basis for division and much heated debate. In a sermon entitled 'The repentance of believers', preached in Londonderry in 1767, Wesley dealt with the enthusiasm of early converts who imagined that 'just because sin does not reign it therefore does not remain'. He insisted that every Christian must honestly face up to feelings of pride, obstinacy, hatred, bitterness, and the putting of love for other people or things before God. Both sins of commission and omission are involved. We need to acknowledge that:

'though we watch and pray ever so much, we cannot cleanse either our hearts or our hands. Certainly we cannot, till it shall please our Lord to speak to our hearts again, to speak the second time, 'be clean': and only then the leprosy is cleansed. Then only, the evil root, the carnal mind is destroyed; and inbred sin subsists no more. But if there be no such second change, if there be no instantaneous deliverance after justification, if there be none but a gradual work of God, then we must be content as well as we can, to remain full of sin till death; and, if so, we must remain guilty till death, continually deserving punishment.'

Proceeding in the second part of this same sermon, he showed that God is able to save 'to the uttermost' all that come to him. He went on to quote the 'exceeding great and precious promises' of Deuteronomy 30:6; Ezekiel 36:25-27, 29; Luke 1:68, 74, 75. He encouraged believers to act now: 'Be thou clean! Only believe', and you will immediately find 'all things are possible to him that believes'.

In the third section of the sermon, he emphasises the need for continued repentance and cleansing after conversion when it 'is absolutely necessary, for us to see the true value of the atoning blood as much after we are justified, as ever we did before.' After the crisis of conversion and cleansing, we are conscious of our inability to retain anything we have received and we live trusting Christ as Priest and King. In this way we 'make him a whole Christ, an entire Saviour; and truly to set the crown upon his head.' Such sanctified believers will then see themselves as branches, entirely dependant upon, and drawing their nourishment from, Christ the vine (Jn 15:1).

For Wesley this became the fundamental reason for establishing his religious Societies. He gathered together in groups of 10-12 those who had experienced victory over besetting sins. In these classes they shared their spiritual experiences and encouraged one another in the practice of holiness, 'without which no-one would see the Lord' (Heb 12:14). Wesley detailed in his *Journal* the procedures followed in these class meetings. 'The evil men were detected, and reproved. They were borne with for a season. If they forsook their sins, we received them gladly; if they obstinately persisted therein, it was openly declared that they were not of us.' Those who remained learned to 'bear one another's burdens' and to naturally 'care for one another'. 'Speaking the truth in love', they grew up into him in all things, who is the Head, even Christ.' A later observer says that those who were excluded were those who did not take their religion seriously enough. This included right conduct towards one's neighbour, for holiness concerned both heart and life. Few were disciplined for purely doctrinal views. Actions were more important than words. When established in Christian maturity, they were encouraged to become Band members and in meetings with fellow Christians they were expected to speak 'freely and plainly, the true state of our souls, with the faults we have committed in thought, word, and deed, and the temptations we have felt, since our last meeting.'

In 1786, near the end of his life, Wesley defined holiness in a letter as 'loving God with all our heart and our neighbour as ourselves.' In a letter to an Irish preacher in Co Leitrim some years earlier, he wrote: 'Holiness ... is love to God and our neighbour; the image of God stamped on the heart; the life of God in the soul of man; the mind that was in Christ, enabling us to walk as Christ also walked.' Loving our neighbour meant not only those within the church but also 'throughout the land'. Wesley said 'lose no opportunity of doing good in any kind ... willingly omit no work either of piety or mercy. Do all the good you possibly can to the bodies and souls of men.' This experience came to be referred to as 'Christian Perfection' or 'Perfect Love'. The term was defined as 'signifying that such a person is complete in answering to the end for which God had made them'. Such perfection did not exclude improvement as knowledge increased. It certainly did not exclude error due to ignorance or immaturity.

It did imply that the individual Christian did everything out of a desire to love God or his/her neighbour.

Wesley's discipline among his preachers is illustrated by this letter to Thomas Maxfield in 1762: 'What I most dislike is your limited love to your brethren and to your own society; your want of meekness, gentleness, long-suffering ... your bigotry and narrowness of spirit ... your critical spirit, your proneness to think hardly of all who do not exactly agree with you; in one word, your divisive spirit.' Who would send out such letters today?

The credibility of the modern church will be determined by a recovery of this practice of sincere love by each for all. Past generations have trusted God to do this radical work in their hearts. It is my prayer that this generation will trust God's unchanging promises for a similar cleansing from all sin, and then go on to model perfect love by the enabling power of the indwelling Holy Spirit. May God grant it!

Prayer:
Refining fire, go through my heart,
Illuminate my soul.
Scatter thy life though every part
And sanctify the whole.

Serious about mission

David Cohen

'...let me explain this to you; listen carefully to what I say.' Acts 2:14

The early church in the Acts of the Apostles was motivated by three factors:

commitment to Jesus Christ as Saviour and Lord,
commitment to the Bible as the word of the living God,
commitment to mission that reaches out to the world that is lost without Christ.

Mission is for radicals. Mission is serious and it is part of being a Christian. It is not something we can choose to do or not. If we are followers of Jesus we cannot avoid being committed to mission. He gives his great commission to the church in every age and sends us 'into all the world to proclaim the gospel' (Mt 28:19). Mission is the radical turn around of disciples who have met with the risen Christ. Conversion is a prerequisite for mission. This is the pattern of the Acts of the Apostles where the enablers of mission were ordinary people (Acts 6:5) who were filled with the Holy Spirit. In terms of mission and evangelism, unless we are converted God will not use us effectively in mission. Mission is for radicals who take Jesus seriously and believe his gospel is for the world, not just for the church. It is about changing sinful individuals and changing sinful society. It is about making sure that every person on this planet hears about Jesus and his love and forgiveness. It believes that God is serious when he says he wants to make people disciples from all nations. Mission is making your life count in the best possible way.

When I became a Christian I heard the call of God to mission by reading stories of people like Amy Carmichael and her vision of blind people hurtling over a cliff while Christians sat in a circle making daisy chains. I read about A. B. Simpson, who prayed with his arms around a globe of the world, weeping for a world lost in sin. Another model was C. T. Studd, the England cricketer who later served God in China and the Congo and founded the Worldwide Evangelisation Crusade with the motto: 'If Jesus Christ be God and died for me then no sacrifice can be too great for me to make for him.' They had a passion for Jesus and a passion for souls. They were brought up on the word of God and their call came from the understanding of the word of God which they took seriously. The Christian church today needs that passion restored.

Mission is urgent. One can sense the urgency in the preaching of Peter in this sermon on the day of Pentecost '... let me explain this to you; listen carefully to what I say' (Acts 2:14). Mission is urgent today because there are people outside the church who are knocking at the door. Many would not recognise Jesus if he came to them today because they have knowledge only of a caricature of Jesus received from films, satire and TV. Yet there is spiritual hunger that is unsatisfied. There is more wealth and knowledge than ever but less passion and less satisfaction. In our 'me' generation, where comfort and tolerance are gods of our age, we need to hear from the church a certain sound as to what is right and what is wrong, because the foundations of society are being shaken as absolutes have been removed. In the pressure to conform to the prevailing ways of the world, Christians have a very powerful, liberating two-letter word called 'no' and we should use it more. The Christian can say, 'No, I will not conform to the ungodly mores of the age, because I am serious about Christ.'

Mission is concerned about transforming society as well as individuals. I am acquainted with a programme called 'Operation Dawn' in some countries of South East Asia where it offers an effective drug rehabilitation programme that is drug-free and Christ-centred. It is a mentoring process where former addicts who are now set free can spend 24 hours a day with the addicts who come in for treatment, care and love. One national government has given an award to this Christian organisation because of its success in treating addicts. We need to believe that today the risen Christ gives the resources and power of the Holy Spirit if only we will draw on them.

Let us examine the sermon of Peter on the day of Pentecost in Acts 2:14-41. Peter, until recently a coward when he denied the Lord, was now preaching the first Christian sermon with boldness in Jerusalem. He was radical, serious and urgent about mission.

The context of mission is the word of God

The scriptures are the key to mission because the knowledge of Jesus spreads as the scriptures are taught. Peter is serious about scripture. His sermon in Acts 2 is based on quotes from the prophets, Psalms and the teachings of Christ. Joel the prophet (v 17-21) speaks about the outpouring of God's spirit on all kinds of people in the last days. We are living in the dispensation of the Holy Spirit who is available and present to men and women and young people (v 17) in the church in every age. If Peter thought that two millennia ago they were living in the last times, then certainly we are. The Lord is coming again when we will least expect him and modern climatic changes make the signs of darkened sun and blood-red moon (v 20) more credible. The purpose of the outpouring of the Holy Spirit is that everyone who calls upon the name of the Lord will be saved (v 21). Peter was experiencing the scripture promises which he was preaching. Believers rooted in the word of God blossom.

The content of mission is Jesus, the living word of God

Peter is also passionate about Jesus. Jesus is the focus of Peter's message. He says: v 22 'Jesus of Nazareth was a man accredited by God to you by miracles, wonders and signs which God did among you through him as you yourselves know.' Peter appeals to their memory and what they had seen. The cross and the resurrection are the focus of the good news about Jesus and the motivation for mission. Anything we need to know about God we find in Jesus for in him all the fullness of God dwells (Col 1:19). Peter then quotes the written word to reveal the living word (v 25) and from the book of Psalms recalls how David's heart and speech were glad and he was filled with hope (v 27). This shadowy hope of the Old Testament is now clearly revealed in the resurrection of Jesus Christ from the dead. Peter concludes with deep assurance in (v 36) with 'Therefore' and we need to ask what the therefore is there for. Because Peter has outlined scriptural passages which point to Jesus as both Lord and Christ he declares: 'Therefore let all Israel be assured of this: God has made this Jesus, whom you crucified, both Lord and Christ'.

The concern of mission is the world

Peter is passionate about the unbelieving world. What happened when Peter opened his heart and preached this radical message? The proclamation of the word of God in the power of the Spirit was life changing for 3000 people at one time. They were cut to the heart (v 37) and in answer to their question they were told to repent and be baptised for the forgiveness of their sins and they would receive the gift of the Holy Spirit. There follows a mission statement of the early church. 'The promise is for you and for your children and for all who are far off, for all whom the lord our God will call' (v 39). This is a world vision and extends to all unreached people. Thousands are being added to the church today and everyday. We are part of a church that is bigger than we think.

The commitment to mission

Peter and the first disciples followed Jesus as he taught them the good news of the kingdom and showed them mission. We are all pilgrims on a journey following Christ as we pass through this world. We can say: 'I'm not now what I used to be, I'm not yet what I want to be, I'm not yet what Jesus is trying to make me, but God is still working in me.' My own desire is to serve Jesus, to become more like Jesus in my life, to accept the scriptures as the living word of God that can change lives and give purpose, guidance and understanding. I don't believe that God is as interested in where we are, where we go and what we do as he is interested in our relationship with him. If I happen by mistake to go North and God wanted me to go South, I'm not sure that God is particularly worried about that because there is work for me to do in the North as in the South. There are other people he can draw on from his radical disciples to go South if I took the wrong turning. What he is wanting is my heart beating in time with his and my commitment subservient to Jesus as my Lord and Saviour. What God wants is our commitment to him in obedience. It may be that next year you will be off to China or the Congo. It may be that God might start to squeeze your wallet or chequebook. Or he might get you on your knees half an hour earlier in the morning to pray.

Prayer:

Our Loving Father, thank you for your written word and Jesus the living Word. Root your word in our hearts that it might bear fruit in changed lives to your glory. Begin with me, then in my family, the church, the community and to the ends of the earth. We ask this prayer in the liberating power and the name of Jesus. Amen.

Keep going!

Ken Wilson

'I press on towards the goal to win the prize.' Philippians 3:14

As a long distance runner I appreciate the need to keep going. Christian service is a marathon and we need the grace and grit to keep going. I want to suggest three main things from Philippians chapter 3 which are really variations on the theme of holiness.

1. Don't Stop!
St Paul says, 'Forgetting the things that are behind … I press on towards the mark' (Phil 3:13-14). St Paul had covered much ground already, but there was still much to learn and many things to be achieved. I fear that too many Christians have given up too easily or they have been too easily satisfied. They have stopped short of the best and too easily seduced by the second best.

Many of the people who have inspired me have been people who have kept going and have never been satisfied with less than the best. They have had such a high understanding of Christian service that they kept reaching for the stars. Like the picture we get of Jesus in Hebrews 12:2, they seem to have had a shining vision before them.

John Wesley has fascinated me for many years. What kept him going? When 10,000 people were converted, he was not satisfied. Even when 30,000, 50,000 were converted he was still not satisfied! Why did he keep on rising at 4.00 am to pray and read his Bible throughout his life? One answer to this question is that Wesley cared little for outward success. He had a passion for holiness. Faithfulness before God was vastly more important than his image in front of others. He believed that there were no limits to what God can do in and through our lives. The early Methodist Societies were like 'schools of holiness' all over the land. They were athletes for God, straining every muscle and every fibre to win the prize. Think of your life as a piece of handwriting done by God. In your life God is writing a new sentence, but it is not yet complete. So be sure you put a 'comma' today and not 'full stop'. He has a lot more to write, no matter how many in-fillings by the Holy Spirit you have received, no matter how many mountaintop experiences, there is still much more. So don't stop.

Don't stop preparing and training! No matter what qualifications we have gained we are still ever beginning. We have not yet arrived at the destination. Don't stop your studies! We are called to be life-long students of the scriptures, of theology, and of life in general. So be inquisitive! Be eager to learn! For there are no limits to what the Lord can do in each one of us.

Don't stop developing your relationship with Christ! Until the day we die – indeed for all eternity – we will keep growing in our understanding of the love and the grace of God. So, pray that you will continually hunger for more of God.

Don't stop developing a sense of wonder and amazement that the Lord has called someone as weak and sinful as you are to serve him! Let verses of scripture turn over in your mind again and again and again. For example, in Ephesians 3:20-21, St Paul does not say, 'Now to him who by the power at work within us is able to accomplish all we can ask or imagine ...' Nor does he even say, 'Now to him who by the power at work within us is able to accomplish far more than all we can ask or imagine ...' He says, 'Now to him who by the power at work within us is able to accomplish abundantly far more than all we can ask or imagine, to him be glory in the church and in Jesus Christ to all generations, for ever and ever.'

While a hunger for God is preferable to a hunger for learning, both are necessary for effective Christian service. We need to keep the vision of our calling bright before us. Daily we must

ask the Lord to open our eyes to see the need around us – and
the need within our own heart.

2. Don't Weaken!

It is always sad when someone's faith and love grow weak and
faint. Jesus says to the church in Ephesus, 'I hold this against
you: You have forsaken (or lost) your first love' (Rev 2:4). Why
do Christian leaders weaken in their faith? Why do we forsake
our first love? I'm sure that we could give dozens of correct answers to these questions. But behind all the reasons is the fact
that something has gone wrong with our personal walk with the
Lord. What you and I are in the private place, where no one but
God sees us, that is what we really are! That is how we find our
true standing with God. And that is far more important than
what we are in the public place, where everyone sees us.

In Matthew 23:16-28 Jesus challenges the religious leaders of
his day. They thought that their image in front of others was
more important than their faithfulness before God. They were
blind and foolish to put such an emphasis on the outside of
things, and yet neglect their hearts. Jesus called them, 'White-
washed tombs, which look beautiful on the outside, but on the
inside are full of dead men's bones and everything unclean' (vv
27-28). You and I will grow weak and feeble if we concentrate on
the outward show of Christianity and fail to ask the Lord to keep
our hearts and minds pure and clean. It is tragic when a minister
of the gospel loses his or her power. My experience is that far too
many busy and gifted ministers are weakened by sin and temptation. Of course, no one wants this to happen. We don't set out
to forsake our first love. We would love to remain in the faith –
strong spiritually. (Later, I will speak about sexual sin. At present I am speaking about our walk with the Lord.)

And yet, so many of us do become weak. This can be brought
on by extreme busyness. You remember what Jesus said in the
Parable of the Sower? He told about some of the farmer's seed
failing to grow because it was choked, 'by the cares of this life
and the deceitfulness of riches' (Mt 13:22). So the cares of life –
committee meetings, administration, visiting, preaching, which

are all good in themselves, can choke the seed of God's word in our hearts. The result is that we become weak and ineffective spiritually, and thus we are no match for the enemy of our souls.

Now, what is the answer to this? Jesus found time to pray, and so must we. Daily prayer and Bible study are vital in the life of the Christian servant if he or she is to be kept strong in the faith. Here is where we get our authority to stand before people to preach and teach the gospel. And here is where sin is dealt with day by day. Here is where we stay fresh and alive through the work of the Holy Spirit. The Apostle Peter once, tragically, denied his Lord because he failed to keep alert. Then, many years later when he was writing to encourage others, he wrote this: 'Be self controlled and alert. Your enemy the devil prowls around like a roaring lion looking for someone to devour. Resist him, standing firm in the faith, because you know that your brothers throughout the world are undergoing the same kind of sufferings' (1 Pet 5:8-9). Peter was speaking out of his own experience. We fight a powerful enemy, therefore we need to spend time every day putting on the whole armour of God (Eph 6:10-20). Pray that the Lord will open your eyes to see whether or not you are weakening. All the resources of heaven are available for us today. Remember, the promise is: 'Ask and you shall receive' (Lk 11:9).

3. Don't Fall

King David fell, (2 Sam 11:1-5); Samson fell, (Jdgs 16:4-20), and the sad day came when St Paul had to say of one of his faithful workers: 'For Demas, because he loved this world, has deserted me' (2 Tim 4:10). You see, when we fall in love with this world's standards and values, we will fall sooner or later!

We have just been speaking about becoming weak in our faith, and one of the serious results of this is that we have no defence against sexual temptation. If the enemy of our souls cannot tempt us to fall in love with money or with power, he will try to tempt us sexually. Of course our sexuality is one of the greatest gifts which God has given us, and when we allow him to sanctify our desires, then our family life and our church life will receive a great blessing. Satan knows this, and therefore will attempt to corrupt this gift from God. For Satan knows the devastating blow this will be to God's Name, and to the work of the church. No Christian sets out to make shipwreck of his or her spiritual life. But wiser and stronger than us have fallen. Sadly, during my ministry I have known gifted gospel preachers who have fallen. The warning from holy scripture is: 'Let him that thinks he stands, take heed lest he fall' (1 Cor 10:12). Also, 'Pride comes before a fall' (Prov 16:18). We need humbly to face up to our weaknesses, and to realise that by ourselves, we are no match for the enemy.

Let me suggest certain steps we can take to avoid falling. (I suggest that you discuss these with your colleagues to see how best they can be adapted to your situation.)

Step 1. Find a 'soul friend' to whom you are accountable. I mean, someone you can trust with your deepest secrets. Arrange that every now and then, say once a month, you will speak with this friend – men with men, and women with women – and agree to search each other's hearts. The early Methodists used to do this in groups in their 'Band Meetings'. Here are some of the questions people had to answer before they were permitted to join 'the Band':

'Do you desire to be told of your faults?'

'Do you desire to be told of all your faults, and that plain and home?'

'Do you desire that every one of us should tell you, from time to time, whatever is in his heart concerning you?'

'Do you desire that, in doing this, we should come as close as possible, that we should cut to the quick, and search your heart to the bottom?'

Step 2. Make up your mind that, even when you are talking about the things of God, you will try not be alone with a member of the opposite sex in a closed room or in a car. Sometimes you can ask another church leader to go with you when called to meet someone in need.

Step 3. If you are married you can speak of your affection for your spouse, when he or she is present or absent.

Step 4. When paying a complement to a member of the opposite sex the emphasis should be on character and conduct, rather than looks.

In the New Testament in the letters to both Timothy and Titus, Paul urges leaders in Christ's church to be above reproach. That is, our conduct must be such that it would be difficult, even for those who try to find fault with us, to bring an accusation against us. Another way of putting all this is that we need to learn to recognise the devil before he springs a surprise on us (2 Cor 2:11).

A final check.

You don't have to stop, but if you have stopped – start again today!

You don't have to weaken, but if you have been weakened – claim the Holy Spirit's power today!

You don't have to fall, but if you have fallen – get up! Seek God's forgiveness today!

Be prepared to face up to the consequences then hear again the call of God to a life of holiness and service.

Prayer:

Lord God, thank you for calling us into this wonderful ministry of preaching and teaching the gospel of Jesus Christ. Pierce my soul with your love that I may long for you with my deepest desire and thirst for you. You are the source of all life, wisdom and light. May I seek you and find you, think on you and speak with you, and undertake all things for the honour and glory of your holy name, for your name's sake. Amen.

Conclusion

'Who is equal to such a task?'
2 Corinthians 2:16

St Paul (in 2 Cor 2:14-3:6) gives some encouraging reasons for confidence and competence in Christian ministry.

We come as we are but we don't stay as we are
We are on a journey. We grow and change as we go. 'Thanks be to God who always leads us in triumphal procession in Christ' (2:14). The victory parades of Roman generals are nothing compared to the triumph of Christ who is our victorious general leading his followers rejoicing in his victory. We may stumble and fall and fail but the victory of the crucified and risen Christ is already secured. His is the kingdom and the power and the glory.

We are together with others on this journey and we learn together the lessons of Christian service. Jealousy between Christians is out of order since the cause, the call and the conquest belong to Christ, not to us.

Little is much if God is in it
People notice us more than we realise. 'I smell gas' is sometimes heard in many households. The truth is that natural gas is odourless and in order to make it safe a very small amount of a chemical called mercaptan n is added to the gas so that gas leaks can be detected. The concentration of mercaptan is very small, only a small part per billion and indeed is so small that it cannot be measured by most chemical techniques. Paul, thinking of the sweet incense from the swinging censers which left the air scented after a passing Roman victory parade, says that our ministry is the aroma of Christ (2:15). It may be miniscule, but it can have a huge impact, for one with God is always a majority and little is

much if God is in it. The perfume industries of Europe often grew up in areas where leather tanning was prevalent, with its pungent smells. I remember, on holiday in Grasse in the South of France, how a strong fragrance filled the air when the workers from the perfume factory emerged into the town for their lunch break. The ministry of Christian workers, who spend time in the presence of Christ, will counteract the bad odours of a decaying world.

'People don't read their Bibles but they read us,' is another comment we hear. 'You are a letter from Christ' (3:3), says Paul. Be encouraged and challenged, your witness is noticed.

The God who calls also equips

Confidence and competence are given. 'Such confidence as this is ours through Christ before God. Not that we are competent in ourselves to claim anything for ourselves, but our competence comes from God. He has made us competent as ministers of a new covenant' (3:4-6).

To those who ask, God gives the Holy Spirit as the supreme resource for Christian service. The Holy Spirit glorifies Christ (Jn 16:14). That is the test of Spirit-filled ministry. To God be the glory!

Prayer:

1 A charge to keep I have:
A God to glorify;
A never-dying soul to save,
And fit it for the sky;

2 To serve the present age,
My calling to fulfil;
O may it all my powers engage
To do my Master's will!

3 Arm me with jealous care,
As in thy sight to live;
And O thy servant, Lord, prepare
A strict account to give!

4 Help me to watch and pray,
And on thyself rely,
So shall I not my trust betray,
Nor love within me die.
Charles Wesley (1707-88) alt.

The Contributors

REV DESMOND BAIN is General Secretary of the Home Mission Department of the Methodist Church in Ireland.

DR BRIAN CALLAN is President of the Royal Society of Chemistry, Republic of Ireland.

REV DAVID COHEN is National Director of Partners International working with Christian Nationals Evangelism Council of Australia. He is a former General Director of Scripture Union in England and Wales.

THE VERY REV PROFESSOR KWESI DICKSON is President of the All Africa Conference of Churches and a former President of the Methodist Church in Ghana.

REV JOHN FARIS is minister of the Presbyterian Churches in Aghada and Cork in the Republic of Ireland.

REV DULEEP FERNANDO is President of the Methodist Church in Sri Lanka.

REV DR PETER C. GRAVES is the minister of Methodist Central Hall, Westminster, London.

REV JOHN HORNER is a retired Methodist Minister and lives in Penzance, Cornwall.

REV DR SINCLAIR LEWIS is a retired District Superintendent Methodist minister in South Carolina, USA.

GILLIAN KINGSTON LIVES IN DUBLIN. She is moderator of the Church Representatives' Meeting of Churches Together in Britain and Ireland.

RT REV HAROLD MILLER is the Church of Ireland Bishop of Down and Dromore.

OSMOND MULLIGAN is a retired consultant surgeon living in Ireland who formerly served in Nigeria.

LYNDA NEILANDS lives in Belfast, is a writer, and is married to David. They have twin boys.

REV CECIL NEWELL is a former President of the Methodist Church in Ireland. He has ministered in Zimbabwe and Ireland.

REV GEARÓID O'SULLIVAN CM is a Vincentian and a chaplain at University College, Cork.

DAVID W. PORTER is Director of E.C.O.N.I. (Evangelical Contribution On Northern Ireland).

CHERIE RITCHIE lives in Dublin, Ireland, and formerly served with her husband Roy in Nigeria.

FERGUS RYAN is leader of Fellowship Bible Church in Dublin and is a retired airline pilot.

REV PROF PETER STEPHENS is a former President of the British Methodist Conference and Professor of Church History at the University of Aberdeen.

REV BRUCE B. SWAPP is Connexional President of the Methodist Church in the Caribbean and the Americas (MCCA).

REV DR NORMAN W. TAGGART is a former President of the Methodist Church in Ireland and served for some years in Sri Lanka.

REV KEN TODD is President-designate of the Methodist Church in Ireland and previously served in Sierra Leone.

REV DR DAVID WILKINSON is an astro-physicist and Methodist minister who lives in Durham, England.

REV DR KEN WILSON is President of the Methodist Church in Ireland and served in the Caribbean.